BRIDGES OF COMPASSION

BRIDGES OF COMPASSION
Insights and Interventions in Developmental Disabilities

Alex Campbell and Lorne Ladner

JASON ARONSON INC.
Northvale, New Jersey
London

This book was set in 11 pt. Galliard by Alabama Book Composition of Deatsville, Alabama.

Library of Congress Cataloging-in-Publication Data

Campbell, Alex R.
  Bridges of compassion : insights and interventions in
  developmental disabilities / Alex Campbell and Lorne Ladner.
      p.   cm.
  Includes bibliographical references (p.   ) and index.
  ISBN 0-7657-0131-6 (alk. paper)
  1. Developmentally disabled children — Mental health — Case studies.
  2. Developmentally disabled children — Rehabilitation — Case studies.
  I. Ladner, Lorne. II. Title.
  RJ507.D48C35 1998
  618.92′85884 — dc21   97-40101

Printed in the United States of America on acid-free paper. For information and catalog write to Jason Aronson Inc., 230 Livingston Street, Northvale, New Jersey 07647. Or visit our website: http://www.aronson.com

Contents

Acknowledgments

Many people contributed directly and indirectly to the evolution of this book. First and foremost, we would like to thank the many clients with whom we've worked over the years. We would also like to thank the direct care staff and administration of the Devereux Foundation. Thanks also to the Mayer Johnson Corporation for their permission to print a number of their icons in this text.

Others whose contributions we would like to acknowledge include: Gary LaVigna, Bill and Barbara Christopher, Ned Christopher, Tom McCool, Kathy Fernberg, Rick Newhouse, the Gibeaut family, Jack Rosenberg, Avedis Panajian, Diane Skafte, Kirk Hoffman, Hans Stahlschmidt, Cathy Piliero, Joyce Mattheson, Scott Kuehn, Omar Noorzad, Wendy Davee, Meredith Sommerville, Charles Nicholson, and Peggy Miller.

On a personal note, we would also like to thank our parents: James and Anne Campbell, Stephen Ladner, and Ronnie Chase. We would also like to thank our wives, Astha Campbell and Theresa Ladner.

Introduction

During our first few years of working with the developmentally disabled at the Devereux Foundation in Santa Barbara, we were able to attend numerous conferences and workshops with researchers, behavioral experts, and leaders in the field. While we were quite interested in current research, we soon came to feel that psychologists, psychotherapists, and others involved in treatment limited themselves by restricting their approach to cognitive-behavioral interventions. We felt that a psychodynamic understanding of what Dr. Gary LaVigna (1996) has referred to as "the person behind the behavior" would open up a richer variety of effective interventions. As newcomers, though, we initially kept these opinions to ourselves.

At this time, one of the authors, while perusing the psychology shelf at a used bookstore, had the good fortune to discover a first edition volume of *Contributions to Psycho-Analysis: 1921–1945* by Melanie Klein (1948), a well-known pioneer in the field of object relations theory. In this book there is a case study of Klein's work with a young client named Dick, who was very similar to many of the autistic clients we had been working with. After purchasing the book, we discovered on the inside cover the signature of the original owner—Helena Devereux Fentress, the founder of the Devereux Foundation, our place of current employment. She had purchased it in the year of its printing, 1948, and had put her personal stamp below her signature; the stamp showed a warm hearth above which were the words *Love Never Faileth*.

This experience inspired confidence in placing less emphasis on *shaping* behavior and in applying ourselves to the psychodynamic *understanding* of behavior. We found that this enhanced understanding could serve as a *bridge*, allowing for increased empathic connection with our clients and for the development of more effective interventions—behavioral and otherwise—to help them live more harmoniously with others. It has been our experience that when an understanding of psychodynamic, developmental, and systemic issues is integrated with the concrete and structured elements of positive behavioral programming, clinical results are enhanced and side effects of treatment are reduced or eliminated.

If connecting different effective approaches was the impetus for this book, a desire to provide *practical and effective interventions* to those who live and work on a day-to-day basis with developmentally disabled children and adolescents was what carried it through to completion. Both of the authors have worked for years with children in various settings who exhibited a wide range of extremely challenging behaviors, and so we are very familiar with the daily struggles of caring family members, teachers, therapists, and group home staff. While we cannot offer any magical or easy solutions to complex problems, we have striven to provide the reader with practical ways of understanding and working directly with developmentally disabled children.

STRUCTURE OF THE BOOK

Each chapter of this book presents a case study that illustrates a particular way of understanding and working with a child or young adult. While protecting the confidentiality of our clients, we have attempted to portray behaviors and the psychological issues that underlie them in as true to life a way as possible. In instances in which interventions were developed over the course of our work with a number of clients, we drew together elements of our experience that would make the material as accessible and practical to the reader as possible.

The book consists of 19 chapters that present a wide range of case material and a variety of interventions. We attempt to make theoretical issues easy to understand for the general reader and have arranged the chapters so that the reader can develop some familiarity with our approach and basic terminology before reaching chapters with more complex issues. Chapter subtitles should be helpful in leading the reader to a theoretical approach or specific behavioral issue that may be of interest.

Technical terms in **bold print** may be looked up in the glossary for further elucidation. The glossary is intended to provide the reader with an understanding of the general meaning of a term and from what theoretical perspective the term is derived. We have also provided several brief appendices that provide a somewhat longer discussion of interventions and points of theory that may be of interest to some readers. A bibliography is also provided for those wishing to do further reading in an area of their particular interest.

THEORETICAL ASSUMPTIONS

Regarding behavioral interventions, we feel that the approach commonly known as **positive programming** is best for clinical, practical, and ethical reasons. The importance of this approach was highlighted for us through an interaction that one of the authors had with an adult autistic client. He was carrying a bag of M&Ms when he arrived at his group home to see another client. When he offered this man, who was in his forties, some of the candy, the man suddenly began shouting, ran to his bedroom, slammed the door, and hid behind his bed. It was later discovered that he had been part of a behavioral treatment program at a major American university where he had received M&Ms as reinforcers when he exhibited desired behaviors but had been locked in a restrictive setting as a punishment when he exhibited undesired behaviors. Although they had been trying to shape his behaviors using punishment, what they had successfully done was to teach him to fear anyone who offered him that particular brand of candy.

This story illustrates how reliance on punishment or negative consequences to change behaviors can create long-term side effects. The side effects of behavioral programs involving punishment becomes even more evident when one has an understanding of clients' psychosocial development and needs. This point is illustrated in Chapter 12, where the use of negative consequences to change negative behaviors is seen to actually increase some of those behaviors while also having significant negative effects on a father–son relationship.

Thus we have come to believe that consequence-based programming is counter-productive and at times detrimental to the well-being of the client. We have found that even extremely challenging behaviors can be dealt with on a short- or long-term basis by a positive programming approach with a multi-element plan that enhances the individual's quality of life.

A key component of positive programming is a **functional analysis** of challenging behaviors. This involves collecting and analyzing data about the specifics of a behavior, with a focus on its antecedents and its consequences in the environment in which it occurs, in order to better understand what *function* or *purpose* the behavior serves. Once the purpose of the behavior has been ascertained, one can teach the disabled person more adaptive ways of achieving that purpose. This process is described in Chapter 2, where we discover that a young man's going AWOL and being aggressive have the function of putting distance between himself and people or stimuli with which he cannot cope. The intervention plan involves alternatives such as his voluntarily going to a "secret" hiding place or putting on his headphones and listening to music.

Although we value the utility of functional analysis, we strongly believe that there are inherent limitations in the standard range of functions or motivations that are ascribed to behaviors. This kind of an approach is essential to long-term success with the developmentally disabled. However, the motivations underlying behavior are much more varied and complex than this approach recognizes, and so other theoretical viewpoints are needed for a more complete understanding of any behavior in question. An in-depth discussion of this point is undertaken in Chapter 3, regarding attention seeking and the importance of understanding the kinds of attention that are being sought.

There is currently a strong movement in this field toward *normalization*. This positive trend attempts to ensure that those with disabilities have access to the same kinds of education, leisure activities, social opportunities, and work experiences as nondisabled peers. We feel that this trend toward normalization must now also be applied to the clinical realm. When a child is diagnosed with a Pervasive Developmental Disorder or with Mental Retardation, there is a tendency to minimize or not see other forms of psychopathology such as anxiety, depression, or the substrates of a personality disorder. This is referred to (Pfeiffer and Baker 1994) as **diagnostic overshadowing.** The developmental diagnosis becomes the central focus and other problems are overlooked. In Chapter 10 we address the histrionic behavior of a child based on our understanding of how elements or precursors of the histrionic personality disorder impact her behaviors.

Behavioral analysis and specific behavioral methods such as discrete trial learning and differential reinforcement are extremely useful and, at times, essential for treatment. However, particularly when working with children, there is no substitute for genuine human warmth and compassion. Throughout this book, we make reference to the importance of empathy, which is a technical term referring to the ability to put aside one's own preconceptions and personal concerns in order to be available to the needs and emotional states of another. Understanding how a child may use autistic encapsulation (Chapter 5) or projective identification (Chapter 11) can help one to see beyond the external behaviors and to understand the inner conflict or pain that the child may be expressing or avoiding. Insights into the causes of behaviors help us to overcome obstacles to empathy, and this lays the groundwork for genuine compassion, which is essential in helping those with developmental disabilities. Although specific treatment plans do not always succeed, loving presence and compassion will carry families, caregivers, and individuals with disabilities across many developmental challenges and obstacles to social integration.

1

TAKING THE BITE OUT OF TEASING:

Covert Reinforcement Helps a Girl Cope with Teasing

I was on my way to the Carrillo program to consult with a staff member about a young, autistic boy when I heard screaming from the back yard. I ran around the side of the house and through a gate in the fence, I immediately saw a commotion in and around the jacuzzi—water splashing, two staff shouting, and a child crying.

Upon my arrival, I saw that Joni, a pretty, 13-year-old girl, had a peer's arm in her mouth. As the peer, a slightly smaller girl, tried to pull away, Joni bit harder. One could see a bruise forming already and a bit of blood on Joni's lower lip. One staff member was trying to keep the girl who was being bitten from pulling away too quickly. The other staff pulled Joni toward her and grabbed hold of her nose. They'd been taught this method of forcing someone to release a bite; the child would let go in order to breathe. But Joni shifted her lower jaw and managed to begin breathing out of the side of her mouth without letting go of her grip.

I moved behind Joni and grabbed hold of her shoulder and head. She was almost hyperventilating. I tried to firmly but slowly pull her away from the other girl. At first there was no movement. Then suddenly she released her grip.

Her mouth opened wide for a few deep breaths and sobs. The staff quickly pulled the other girl out of the jacuzzi. The moment Joni caught her breath, she looked down and was shocked to find that the arm she'd been biting was gone.

She quickly spun around, slipping out of our grasp, her open mouth heading for my leg. Holding her forehead and the side of her face, I was able to hold her off, a few inches from my leg. Her mouth remained wide open; she was sobbing and still trying to bite down on my leg. Then quickly she turned to try to bite my arm. Again I was barely able to move and hold her off. One of the other staff then came and grabbed hold of one of her arms. Cautiously, we pulled her out of the water.

Over an hour later, when Joni had calmed down, I asked one of the staff who had been there throughout the incident what had happened. She explained that Joni's peer, Liz, had been splashing water and laughing—a kind of self-stimulatory play. Joni had turned to Liz, screaming. Liz, caught up in her own play, hadn't noticed Joni's scream but had continued laughing. Joni had clearly taken this as teasing and immediately became enraged, grabbing Liz, shouting at her, and then biting her arm.

I spoke with a number of other people who worked with Joni, and it became clear that any time Joni felt someone was teasing her, she become so enraged that she would become aggressive, losing control of herself for between 30 and 90 minutes. During a number of these incidents she had injured staff and peers by biting, hitting, or pushing them. The staff also explained that they'd tried a number of behavioral contracts and interventions with Joni unsuccessfully. They and their supervisor asked for a consultation on a plan to help decrease these severely aggressive behaviors.

I began by reviewing the interventions that had been tried up to that point. What I found was that most were designed either to reward Joni for not becoming aggressive or to take away privileges and rewards for becoming aggressive. They also involved counseling her after incidents. Conversations with Joni's parents indicated that this was a longstanding behavior.

A conversation that I had with Joni herself was most important. I asked Joni how she felt about herself in relation to her aggressive tantrums. When asked about them, she looked down with what seemed to be genuine embarrassment and said, "That stinks; no good." Both Joni's parents and the staff who had been working with her confirmed that she did seem to genuinely regret these incidents after they were over. Two staff who knew her well said that she would cry afterwards, expressing sincere regret.

As I continued talking with people who knew Joni and reviewing the documented reports of past incidents, it became clear that her behavior was not entirely intentional. Joni was diagnosed as having Pervasive Developmental Disorder, NOS, which implies significant deficits in the *understanding* of interpersonal interactions.

Recent research has shown that people with Pervasive Developmental Disorders have unusual deficits in the ability to understand others' feelings, thoughts, and desires. For example, one successful author and speaker with a Pervasive Developmental Disorder reports that she was unable to understand why it would be advantageous to use humor or interesting anecdotes in her speeches to maintain an audience's interest. This illustrates the difficulty people with these diagnoses have in understanding the needs, feelings, and expectations of others. It is no wonder that a lifetime of difficulty understanding social cues and the motivations of others also leads to significant problems in developing a functional range of appropriate responses for various interpersonal interactions.

As I familiarized myself with Joni's history and observed her social interactions, it became increasingly clear that she very much wanted to be able to relate with others and take part in social interactions. But, because of her developmental disability, she often misunderstood others' intentions and reacted in ways that alienated her from others. The incident at the jacuzzi was one of the more extreme examples of a misunderstanding that led to a severe behavioral problem.

My assessment revealed that the behavioral plans that had been tried with Joni had actually exacerbated the problem. Her staff's intent in using these interventions was to teach Joni that these behaviors were unacceptable by giving a negative consequence in response to them. But this was missing the point. Joni already felt that her behavior was bad. What she needed was an expanded repertoire of choices when faced with someone who she felt was "teasing" or "being mean" to her. The consequences she'd received for acting out in these situations did not teach her to react differently. They were actually understood by Joni as indicating that she was *bad*, increasing her feelings of frustration, isolation, and her negative self-image.

So, working with her staff, I developed a new intervention plan for Joni, using a special form of **covert reinforcement** designed for use with the developmentally disabled. According to this new plan, Joni would not receive formal consequences (i. e., loss of privileges) for her aggressive behaviors for the reasons given above. Instead, after aggressive incidents, staff would talk with Joni about alternative ways that she could have reacted in the antecedent situation and role play her alternative reactions (using elements of the imagery rehearsal sequence described below). If her staff did not feel safe having Joni take part in a specific activity such as an off-campus outing due to her agitation or a recent aggression, they would present this to Joni honestly, explaining their concern for her and everyone's safety rather than presenting it as a punitive reaction to her aggressive behavior.

One aspect of Joni's intervention plan was a contingency contract or progressive schedule of **differential reinforcement**. We designed this contract to ensure that Joni would be receiving positive recognition and social attention for interacting well with others. Too often, developmentally disabled children receive more attention for their negative behaviors than they do for positive ones, and this does not escape their attention!

The most important element of Joni's new plan was our use of *imagery rehearsal* to teach her a new way of reacting when she felt others were teasing or being mean to her. We used a sequence of pictures along with a script as illustrated in Figure 1–1. The picture in each of the eight boxes appeared on the front of an index card, with the script/instructions to staff on the back, so that as they held up the picture for Joni to view they could also read the script.

This is a proactive rather than a reactive intervention. This means that staff would engage in it with Joni daily at a time when she was calm and doing well. The staff would show Joni each picture in order,

hanging out

"You are hanging out with your friends—"
Have her identify a specific activity she'll
imagine they're doing.

peer teasing

"And someone teases you."
Have her identify a specific peer she'll
imagine as the teaser for this session.

upset

"You feel upset."
You can ask her how she looks or feels
when she's upset.

stop

"So, you stop."

Figure 1–1

deep breath

"And you take a deeeep breath."
Practice taking a deep breath with her.

talk with staff

"And you tell staff what has happened."
Have her identify specific staff and imagine
telling them what's happened. Ask what she'd
tell them.

staff helps

"Staff helps."
Have her imagine what staff does to help.

proud

"And you feel really proud of yourself for doing
a very good job and handling this maturely."
Have her imagine staff praising her for doing well and
imagine the positive feelings she'll have about herself
for handling things well.

reading the script and briefly discussing each step with her. In general, the sessions were brief (approximately 10 minutes) and enjoyable, even playful for Joni and the staff.

This kind of structured, consistent, repetitive teaching interaction has proven to be very effective for people with developmental disabilities. Using the pictures and having students gradually learn to say more and more of the script themselves and actually practice the reactions described is very effective in helping them to develop and use the new skills in real-life situations.

On one occasion, I witnessed an interaction between Joni and a peer in which the peer took a doll away from her and called her "stupid." Joni suddenly stopped, looked away, took a very deep breath, and then marched over to staff to report what had occurred.

Over the next few months, Joni's aggressions gradually decreased from an average of 1.5 per week to a point where she was going for periods of four to six weeks without any aggressive episodes. Also, staff reported that her ability to relate positively with peers was improving. As the imagery rehearsal format was seen to be so effective with Joni, additional sequences were developed to help her to build additional new skills in other areas of her life as well, and her aggressive behaviors continued to decrease in frequency and duration.

2

YOU'VE GOT THE POWER:

Michael Helps Create His Own Anger Management Program

When Michael was assigned to me for counseling, I was told by his prior therapist that he hated both group and individual sessions and, regardless of consequences, he would show up once a month at best.

It was no surprise then that our first meeting began with a wild struggle at my door, as Michael tried to break free from the two staff who had accompanied him.

"I don't want to see no new counselor! Let me go! I want to see Christina instead!"

Christina was his former counselor, who had somewhat prepared me for the struggle that was ensuing. Finally the staff coaxed him into my office with a promise of a trip to McDonald's. Michael met my gaze briefly with a sullen look, and refused to say a word. My first impression was of a good looking, African-American, 14-year-old who was depressed. I was to learn later that his verbal skills masked severe cognitive deficits.

The staff who had brought Michael promised to wait outside the door in the event of behavior problems, which they told me typically included physical aggression, property destruction, and prolonged screaming. I told them to return to the classroom, and I sat with Michael in silence.

After a few minutes he became fidgety and, looking at me suspiciously, asked, "What do I get for coming here?"

I ran through some treat and privilege options lightheartedly, and then asked him what he thought counseling was all about.

"*You're* supposed to know that," he mumbled, and then added, "Why do you just sit there not saying anything? Christina was nicer than you. She gave me lots of treats."

With children like Michael it is essential for rapport building not to trigger oppositional-defiant tendencies or get into power struggles. I had been told by staff that the most important thing to do was set firm limits with clear consequences, so that he knew who was in charge. "Take control from the start, and avoid being manipulated," was their motto.

But I have found it highly ironic, even absurd, that experienced direct care staff and licensed clinicians in this field find themselves at risk of being manipulated by mentally retarded individuals. The more experienced the staff, it seems, the greater their fear of out-of-control behavior and manipulation.

Why not avoid the power struggle from the outset by attuning to affect and the child's immediate emotional need? What this means is that you need to initially set aside behavioral goals, the past negative experience of others, and therapeutic theories or agendas in order to simply be energetically present and open to the communicated needs of the child. If you force or cajole an angry or depressed child through a complex ritual of demands, rewards, and consequences, you may get the desired behavior but miss the opportunity to understand the developmental injuries, deficits, and individual pain underlying the problematic behavior.

After several months of telling me that I was mean and that counseling was stupid, Michael finally told me why he didn't like coming to his appointments.

"I don't like being in a room alone with someone," he muttered, looking away.

I asked him if it was someone in particular, or just anyone. When he said it was with men, I reminded him that he had also refused to see Christina. And then guessing that the time might be right, I posed the question, "What happened to you when you were in a room alone with someone when you were little, Michael . . . before you came here . . . when you were still living with your mom?"

Michael's face contorted and he threw a pillow at the wall, followed by a Power Ranger and a wad of Play-Doh.

"Well, I was in this motel with my sister, and my mom had a big fight with this guy. He started beating on my mom, and bottles and things were getting smashed. He just kept beating on her and she was screaming, and my sister was screaming, and the cops came and took me and my sister away. Goddammit, they didn't have to take me away from my mom, Goddammit! Cops are motherfuckers! They didn't have to do that! You've got to help me find my mom!"

Michael is one of many children in this society born to parents with alcohol and drug problems. These children are often physically and/or sexually abused, and many suffer from extreme physical and emotional abandonment. In Michael's case, his ability to cope was further impaired by cognitive deficits that made it difficult for him to understand the world he lived in. To compensate, Michael created a grandiose fantasy realm in which he intended to become "a Kung Fu champion, the strongest and fastest man in the world—better than Schwarzenegger!"

One day Michael showed up for his appointment at 12:30, and when I told him he was an hour and a half late, he insisted that it was 11 o'clock. I showed him the time on my watch, but he simply shook his head. I called in three colleagues and showed him the time on their watches, but Michael was not impressed. I then attempted to reason with him, pointing out that he had already finished lunch, which was always after his regular appointment time. But Michael stuck to his guns. He sat down on the floor outside my door and stated, "It's 11 o'clock, I made my appointment. I ain't movin' until I get my treat! You promised I'd get my treat!"

I resisted the impulse to call staff and have him walked back to class. I decided instead to simply tolerate his abrasive, demanding manner and his outrageous insistence on a skewed perception of reality. Later in the day during a quiet moment, I reflected that I make this type of accommodation automatically with my wife, friends, fellow psychotherapists, and even casual acquaintances who affect my life—so why not for Michael?

I had to adjust my schedule as well as my therapeutic expectations with Michael, and accept progress in micro-steps. With diagnoses of Oppositional-Defiant Disorder and Moderate **Mental Retardation**, a history of physical and sexual abuse, and a mother who had abandoned him, Michael was a clinical challenge, to put it mildly. He expressed the way he felt about how life had treated him by way of 30–60-minute tantrums that involved property destruction and physical aggression toward anyone within reach.

Due to the severity of Michael's acting-out behavior, it was essential to formulate and implement a *behavioral intervention plan* in conjunction with his counseling. Caregivers in any setting always need a great deal of support, and the best kind of support to give is a way of decreasing severe problem behaviors as soon as possible.

The first step in decreasing problem behavior is to collect data relevant to the *antecedents* of the *target behavior* in order to help all parties involved in a client's care understand the function or underlying cause of the behavior. This is often referred to as the *communicative intent* of the behavior. The following steps are a simple guide for doing what is called a *functional analysis* of problem behavior.

Step 1: Study and summarize the written behavioral reports.

If, in any setting, this is not being done, it is essential that whoever is in charge of the treatment plan makes sure this does get done. As Michael was in a well-managed residential setting, this information was available.

Step 2: Collect anecdotal information from key individuals in both residential and educational settings.

It is important to speak to as many people as possible to get a total picture. This group will include teachers, speech therapists, the school principal, on-line staff, supervisors, assistant supervisors, volunteers, as well as family members and funding agency representatives when possible.

I was quite disconcerted by the variation in the way well-trained staff perceived Michael. He was described as "mean," "lazy," and "a thief," even though he was ostensibly well liked by many in both educational and residential settings. Their hearts were in the right place, but their lack of understanding made their interactions with Michael ineffective, and more often than not *created* behavioral problems.

Step 3: Carefully review prior behavioral treatment plans and medical records, particularly if medication is a primary component of treatment.

There are times when a medication change can be a highly relevant antecedent to behavioral change. With Michael this was not an issue.

Step 4: Get agreement on a simple operational definition of the problem that is being addressed.

Everyone agreed that Michael's violent tantrums were the problem, but he also had verbal outbursts and sullen moods, delighted in profane invective, and would sometimes argue interminably. A tantrum can mean many things to many people, and so it was important that everyone working with Michael know exactly what the treatment plan was addressing. In many group homes and special education classes phrases such as *extreme aggression, appropriate behavior, unfriendly behavior* are still quite common, but are counterproductive. With most **dually diagnosed** children and adolescents you must be very specific and concrete. So it was important to define the presenting problem to both Michael and staff as any incident involving hitting, kicking, spitting, breaking things, and throwing hard objects.

Behavioral analysis also addresses the *frequency, intensity,* and *duration* of behavior. In Michael's case, his tantrums occurred an average of 4 times per week, so frequency was not so much an issue as the duration and intensity of the episodes, which often lasted over an hour.

Step 5: Determine the antecedents of the targeted behavior.

Antecedents are anything that happens prior to the behavior. Included here are: behaviors of client, behavior of peers, time of day, activities, attitudes of staff, food issues, and aspects of the physical environment. (Physical and emotional indicators are referred to as *precursors* and are intimately linked to antecedents.) In Michael's case the readily identifiable antecedents were *demands* by staff and *verbal conflicts with peers and staff.*

Step 6: Understanding the communicative intent or underlying causes of the behavior.

Given Michael's history of abuse it was clear that he felt easily invaded and threatened. Routine demands of life presented to him by staff were taken by Michael as an impeachment of his personal autonomy. He would dispute matters of simple fact, as illustrated above, as if his life depended on being right. His extremely low self-esteem made it difficult for him to cope with any kind of criticism, teasing, or offhand remark.

It was important for all those interacting with Michael to understand this so that they would be capable of greater empathy, and would be able to intervene more effectively.

Step 7: Involve the client to whatever degree possible in the intervention plan.

Given Michael's verbal skills, the following treatment plan was formulated (see Figures 2–1 and 2–2), using Michael's own words whenever possible. Michael decided on the name of this treatment plan after serious deliberation. He also completed the first draft on a computer during one of his counseling sessions.

The most important aspect of this program is the specification of options for Michael so that when he feels hurt, angry, and disposed to retaliatory behavior he can make choices or be offered choices by caregivers. The reinforcement schedule works in the following way.

Figure 2–1

MICHAEL'S LIFE

(Anger management program)

ANTECEDENTS   *LIVE TIME RESPONSE*

(To hitting, kicking, spitting, stabbing,
breaking things, throwing hard objects)

1. Being bugged by staff . . . . Take deep breaths
   (staff requests and demands)

2. Lies and rumors . . . . Walk away / talk to staff

3. Name calling and teasing . . . . Ignore / talk to staff

4. Being ignored (staff not paying . . . . Go to room, and get
   attention or listening)   *I need to talk with you* card.

OTHER OPTIONS: Use pass to go for walk to education building.
                 Use pass to go to local tennis court area.
                 Go to room and listen to quiet music.
                 Write in journal.
                 Draw in special drawing book.

Figure 2-2

REINFORCEMENT SCHEDULE

Stage	Interval *	Step-up Criterion **	Reward ***

Stage 1 . . . .30 minutes . . . . .8/10 successful trials . . . . .banana and drink

Stage 2 . . . .30 minutes . . . . .8/10 successful trials . . . . .banana and drink
or time with staff

Stage 3 . . . .1 hour . . . . .8/10 successful trials . . . . .25 cents or
time with staff

Stage 4 . . . .2 hours . . . . .8/10 successful trials . . . . .50 cents or
time with staff

*This program will be run 2 times per shift, and data will be recorded on sheet provided.

**The re-start method will be used. This means that as soon as Michael does not earn his reward 3 times in any sequence of 10 trials, he starts over again.

***Michael will be given 2 prompts or reminders in any situation and still earn his reward.

During any stage, staff will say to Michael, "This is *your life!*" Or, "It's Michael's Life—live from California!"

This is to cue Michael that for the specified interval (30, 60, or 120 minutes), he's "on stage" and will earn the stated reward for engaging in the "Live Time Response" behaviors rather than the aggressive behaviors listed.

When the interval is over, staff will discuss with Michael what happened during this time. Thus he gets to work for increasingly more motivating rewards, and has the opportunity for more personal contact with staff. The rewards are selected by Michael, and known by staff to be motivators.

This is an example of a fairly standard **DRO** (differential reinforcement of other behavior) schedule that may be adapted for other children and adolescents at a comparable functional level.

Michael became increasingly invested in his anger management program because he had helped create it and could make modifications when appropriate. He was proud of himself when he was able to walk away a from a conflictual situation rather than lash out in a destructive way. His aggression decreased significantly as he came to feel that he had the power to successfully deal with the negative features of his environment in ways that brought him both external and internal rewards.

3

WHEN ATTENTION IS AN EMERGENCY:

Psychosocial Development and Attentional Needs

I recall one rainy Monday in late winter, when the weather was still quite cool, I was looking out the window during a break between therapy sessions. My office at the time overlooked a group home for which I was providing behavioral consultation.

I was surprised to see all ten clients together with their caregivers, filing hurriedly out into the rain; many did not have jackets on as they tried to huddle together beneath just two umbrellas. They all walked about sixty feet from the building and stood together in the cold rain. I listened more closely through the sound of the rain, and I could just barely hear the sound of a fire alarm coming from inside their house.

In a later session with one of the residents, I learned that they'd had to file out into the cold rain two more times that evening. When I asked my client what had happened, he said, "Danny—stupid Danny—keeps pulling the fire alarm."

Danny was a 14-year-old boy with Mental Retardation in the Mild to Moderate range and very limited expressive verbal skills. He knew a few words in sign language and used picture cards to identify chosen items or activities. He had only been at this group home for a little over three months, and his caregivers had recently mentioned to me that he'd just begun to feel comfortable in this setting, his first out-of-home placement.

Now Danny had begun exhibiting a new behavior: he would pull the fire alarm and then, when staff came running to get him, he would laugh at the "show." Over the next few days, this behavior continued at a rate of three to four times per evening. As the rains continued, Danny's joyous reaction in the face of others' obvious annoyance was not increasing his popularity.

That Thursday evening, two exasperated, soaking caregivers appeared in my office asking for input on a new behavioral plan for Danny. I asked them why they thought that Danny had begun pulling the fire alarm. Without hesitation, both simultaneously said, "Attention!"

In home, educational, and residential care settings alike, the need that many developmentally disabled children have for attention presents a very real challenge. When a functional analysis of challenging behaviors is done, it is often found that attention seeking is a major reason for these behaviors. However, this information alone is often not very useful in developing a treatment plan. The multiple demands on parents' time in home settings and the staff-to-client ratios in school and group home settings limit the attention available for any one child.

To address challenging behaviors that involve attention seeking, it can be useful to understand the various specific kinds of attention and care that children may be seeking. Focusing solely on the child's overt behaviors and environmental antecedents and consequences, we run the risk of not seeing the pyschosocial *developmental needs* that may underlie these behaviors. It has sometimes struck me that just as Eskimos have many words corresponding to the various kinds of snow, those who wish to work effectively with the developmentally disabled must have an understanding of the many kinds of attention that these children may need.

Throughout this book, you will find that children who exhibit ostensibly attention-seeking behaviors are seen as expressing significant psychodynamic developmental needs that must be addressed. One child may need quiet, empathic **mirroring**, another may need well-thought-out feedback, and still another may need more dramatic and intense opportunities to be seen and heard. By designing intervention plans with an awareness of the child's individual developmental needs, better long-term results are achieved and side effects are minimized.

In looking closely at Danny's needs for attention, we found a few factors that were very important in developing an effective intervention. First, we noticed that he did not always want attention. He would often spend up to fifteen or twenty minutes alone playing with a toy or exploring the house or yard. We found that a majority of the incidents of fire alarm pulling had occurred just after he'd spent some time alone. We also found that when Danny did want attention, he often wanted lots of it. His excitement when people came running with much ado after his pulling the fire alarm was a function of this desire.

Danny would also jump around on the living room furniture, dance in the living room, or run out the front door as if to run away in order to draw intense attention to himself. The final thing that we noticed regarding Danny's desire for attention was that he did not seem to differentiate between what we would think of as positive and negative kinds of attention; he seemed to enjoy the attention he got when people were upset about his pulling the fire alarm as much as he enjoyed the attention he received when staff would play music and dance together with him in the living room.

Based on these observations, we hypothesized that Danny was struggling with developmental issues related to what Margaret Mahler (1968) has identified as the **separation-individuation** phase of development, which generally occurs in normal children between ages 6 months and 2 years. An important aspect of this developmental stage is that the child becomes increasingly curious about the outer world while still very much needing to return to the parent for emotional **refueling** (Gabbard 1994). Another important factor during this stage of development is the child's growing recognition of the parent as a separate individual with her own moods and emotions. The child's new awareness of himself as separate leads to "awareness of vulnerability" and "dependence on the mother" (Hamilton 1988).

Our impression was that Danny had never succeeded in consolidating his sense of self as separate from his parents as fully as most nondisabled peers would have done. Then, his coming to an out-of-home placement had heightened his feelings of vulnerability and his fear of abandonment. His curiousity about his environment and his increasing sense of comfort in his new home were healthy. However, the fragility of his sense of self and his underlying dependency needs and fears of abandonment would sometimes be triggered when he was apart from staff, leading to his pulling the fire alarm or to the other behaviors that would bring him the intense attention he was needing to allay his anxieties. The intensity of the attention he sought seemed to reflect the intensity of the anxiety he wished to alleviate.

Based on our understanding of Danny's developmental needs, we came up with a few practical, straightforward interventions. The staff who worked with Danny encouraged him to continue spending time alone playing or walking in safe areas when he wanted to do so. However, they began checking in on him every 10–15 minutes to remind him that he was welcome to join the group. The intent here was to be supportive and to allay anxiety or fears of abandonment. They taught him that whenever he wanted attention, he could wave at staff and gesture for them to come closer. If he did this, then the staff showed him that they would indeed consistently come over and give him a few minutes of attention.

Then, we created a simple contract with Danny for not pulling the fire alarm as illustrated in Figure 3–1. The contract ensured that if Danny did not pull the fire alarm, then he could earn three reinforcing, high-attention activities with staff each evening. We created a menu of seven picture cards with velcro on the back, each of which corresponded to an activity such as dancing in the living room, playing on his electric keyboard together with staff, a walk alone with a favorite staff, making a favorite snack, and so on. Each day, just after school, Danny and a caregiver would choose three of these picture cards for that evening and attach them to the contract that hung in his bedroom. At this point, they would remind him verbally, while pointing at the pictures on the contract, that if he asked appropriately and didn't pull the fire alarm, he would receive one-on-one time with staff doing these fun activities.

Figure 3–1

DANNY'S CONTRACT

If Danny

Does <u>Not</u>

Pull the Fire Alarm

He Earns:

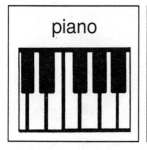

During the first few days of this contract's implementation, Danny did pull the fire alarm at least once per evening. Each time that he did so, his caregivers dealt with him in a matter-of-fact fashion. As soon as they could return to the house, they took him to his bedroom and verbally expressed disappointment at his not having come to them to ask for attention appropriately. They then pointed to the pictures on the contract, indicating that he had not earned one of his three reinforcing activities. When he went for a period of one and a half to two hours without pulling the fire alarm, a caregiver would take him to his room and praise him excitedly for doing well, asking him to choose which reinforcing activity he wanted to engage in. He would choose by pulling one of the pictures from the contract and would immediately be given the opportunity to engage in that activity with his caregiver.

Within fourteen days, Danny had completely stopped pulling the fire alarm. He also seemed happier, as his relations with staff and peers were improving. As he clearly enjoyed his contract, after three weeks we changed the criteria for success from not pulling the fire alarm to not leaving the dorm without asking, using a picture card that we developed for this purpose. Over the following months, he began consistently asking for permission before leaving the dorm, which allowed staff to more easily ensure his safety. Danny also began actively asking for attention by waving to the staff.

What we found generally was that this contract helped Danny to differentiate between positive and negative attention. The concreteness of the contract itself combined with the consistently similar responses from different staff when he sought attention appropriately or inappropriately helped him to begin noticing the kinds of changes in his caregivers' feelings and reactions to him that his different behaviors brought about. Although he did continue to tease his caregivers occasionally by gesturing toward a fire alarm or pretending that he was about to leave out the front door, his challenging behaviors continued decreasing, and his interest in learning to use sign language and a growing number of pictures for communication increased steadily over the next few months.

Although Danny's cognitive and language deficits will continue to make dependence an issue for him, over the full two years that I worked with him I saw Danny make significant developmental gains. His anxiety about spending time alone decreased greatly, and he learned to assert autonomy more appropriately. It was also a great pleasure to see how, as his anxiety decreased, he began expressing his sense of humor in a more reciprocal way.

4

A LEGEND
IN HIS LIFETIME:

A Family Systems Tale of the Forest and the Trees

My first encounter with Darrell was serendipitous. I was walking toward a special education class when my attention was drawn to a tall, thin adolescent with black curly hair who was leaping up down and twiddling a drinking straw. Although he was about fifty yards away and I was not looking directly at him, he sensed my attentional shift and came leaping and bounding over to me. He scrutinized me carefully, making an extraordinary grimace. Speaking in a high pitched, nasal tone, he exclaimed, "I'm going to kick Shirley in the head!" He then danced away, laughing and chortling to himself with great delight.

When I made inquiries shortly thereafter, I learned that this was the legendary Darrell, known on the school campus as a "five-man restraint." This meant that when he "went off," it required five staff members to prevent him from being a danger to himself or others. Yet it hardly seemed possible to be true of this slight, impish young man.

Several months later I was asked to create a behavioral program for Darrell, as he had just moved to a new group home. In discussions with staff I learned that they were quite frightened at the prospect of having to deal with his lengthy aggressive episodes; on the other hand, they were fascinated by his savant abilities. For example, if you asked

Darrell the day of the week on January 30, 2003, he could tell you the correct day. His basic greeting (when not an aggressive utterance) was, "What's your birthday?" Once you had stated your birthdate, he would tell you what day of the week you were born.

Darrell's file was enormous, with full documentation of his aggressive behavior over a five-year period, and it was clear that something more than yet another behavioral plan was needed. It appeared that his parents had always been active participants in decisions involving his care and were highly influential at a political level in the field of developmental disabilities. Darrell's mother called him every other day, and visited him twice a month. Darrell's group home staff, who alternately feared and indulged him, seemed to be in a continuous debate as to what medication, reinforcer, and behavioral intervention would help them prevent his aggressive behavior. They also resented Darrell's parents, whom they viewed as demanding and critical of their work. I had no immediate solution to offer. I was really in the woods here, and given the complexities of this case, I decided that a **structural family therapy** approach could help. I felt that the way those involved in Darrell's care related to each other and to Darrell could be contributing to his behavioral problems. I hoped that, with a common understanding and clearly defined therapeutic goals, there might be some separation of the forest from the trees.

Structural family systems work usually begins by assessing the roles and responsibilities of family members, with an emphasis on the allocation of *power* within the family system. This struck me as quite relevant, as there seemed to be a power struggle between parents and care providers. The family structure is also assessed by the type of **boundaries** between family members, which has to do with the frequency and intensity of interaction and how they regulate it.

I arranged a two-hour interview with Darrell's mother and father, with Darrell scheduled to participate at the end. As I listened to them, I was moved by the degree of suffering they had gone through over the years in their attempts to have a positive relationship with their son. I joined with them by commenting on how anxious I might feel if my son were regularly being put in physical restraints. I told them that my concern was not only for Darrell but for them as well, seeing that Darrell's needs and aggressive behavior created a great deal of stress for everyone in the family.

When Darrell came in to join us there was an immediate enactment of the transactional patterns between family members. In systems theory this refers to the automatic ways individuals relate to each other that often create a rigid or "stuck" family dynamic. These patterns arise as a way of coping with life's challenges and are often sustained by the best of intentions. On coming in, as if on cue, Darrell tore up the straw he'd been twiddling, giggled, and kicked his mother, while his father hovered nearby, alternately criticizing his wife's interactions and issuing ineffective commands to Darrell. In fact, they were both critical of each other's way of relating to Darrell, which can be summarized as follows:

> *Father:* You just don't know how to let Darrell know who's in charge. I don't have half the problems you do with him!
>
> *Mother:* That's easy for you to say. Who drives up here every other weekend? Who's been taking the kicks, the punches, spitting, and insults all these years?

Darrell's parents were intense communicators and expressed many concerns about the shortcomings of staff at his group home. As I listened I couldn't help but reflect on staff perceptions that the family interfered with their efforts to help and all they ever heard from them were complaints. It was apparent to me that even though Darrell's family loved him, and staff were committed to helping him, Darrell was the focal point of anxiety, conflict, and negativity in both **subsystems** of his care. The group home functioned as an extension (or subsystem) of the family, and was, in a sense, part of the larger family system. I felt that it was of the utmost importance to address the dynamic between these two groups and its impact on Darrell. By working directly with them I hoped to "unhook" Darrell as the **identified patient**—a primary goal of the structural approach.

As a consultant I was able to give input to the group home and do family therapy as needed. To "unhook" Darrell as the identified patient it was necessary to discover what role he played as the center of attention in his family. I spoke to Darrell's brother and learned that he had just left home a year previously, and like his parents, felt that family closeness was a priority. Subsequent conversations with all family members led me to believe that besides an agreement that they needed to be a close family, they actually had very few common interests. Darrell's parents had separate careers, and as far as I could see, led separate lives. It struck me that the family maintained its closeness through a common concern about Darrell. I felt that athough I was still in the forest, I was beginning to identify some of the trees.

Darrell's role in the family was intimately related to the boundaries that comprised the family system. In structural language, there were rigid boundaries (not much connection) between mother and father, as illustrated by the fact that they spent little time together outside of their concern for Darrell. Their way of relating was actually stiff, formal, and of a utilitarian nature. On the other hand there were diffuse boundaries (not much emotional separation) between Darrell and his mother. She called him every night, and appeared to be in a state of constant concern about the details of his life, from what he ate for dinner to the location of his socks and underwear. Though this was an expression of her love, she conveyed great deal of anxiety to both Darrell and group home staff. With a similar degree of intensity, Darrell monitored the whereabouts of his mother and became very upset if he could not reach her. He also demanded to know intimate details of his brother's life, particularly how much time he spent with his wife, Shirley. It was my hypothesis that family anxiety was channeled through Darrell who, due to his autistic hypersensitivity, amplified the intensity of feeling and acted it out behaviorally.

Darrell's role in the group home soon became similar to that in his family of origin. I was told during one of my consultations that Darrell was having very severe problems at the time, with an increase in the incidence of property destruction. When I later asked Darrell what he felt his problem was, he grimaced, inhaled through his teeth, and waved his twiddler over his head wildly. "I'm upset because of the staffing *prob*lems," he said, "There's staffing *prob*lems because there's not enough money to pay staff. Are *you* going to get fired, too? People get *fired* when there's not enough money. That's why I'm going to do serious property destruction and punch someone in the nose!"

Apparently, Darrell had overheard a serious discussion about layoffs and staff shortages. He had felt the intensity of staff dissatisfaction and anxiety, and acted it out behaviorally. In this way he became "symptom carrier" for a system in crisis.

Consulting with the family and group home on a weekly basis, I gradually shifted the focus of treatment over a three-month period from Darrell to the family and group home subsystems. I felt that I now had a bird's eye view of the *forest*, and defined the task of restructuring the larger system in the following way:

1. Foster less rigid boundaries between Darrell's mother and father (sometimes referred to as the *executive parental sub-system*) by encouraging them to unite as a team in the parental role.
2. Foster less rigid boundaries between father and son by encouraging more contact between them.
3. Decrease mother–son enmeshment by way of communication guidelines and behavioral limit setting as conditions of personal contact.
4. Foster better communication and a common focus between the group home and Darrell's family (the two subsystems).

As is often the case, systems began to function better once problems were discussed openly in an atmosphere of respect and appreciation. As I had assumed the responsibility of facilitating positive dialogue between Darrell's family and the group home staff, I was pleased to see an evolving relationship of trust. Darrell's mother and father came to see that the staff were patient, dedicated, and doing their best to improve Darrell's quality of life. This led to greater cooperation and better communication regarding visits and Darrell's material needs.

The task of decreasing mother–son enmeshment was much more difficult. I had a very hard time convincing Darrell's mother that she needed to differentiate her own anxiety from Darrell's. In spite of improved relations with staff, she would often phone back after Darrell's calls and tell them that her son was anxious and it was urgent they do something about it. She continued to resent the fact that nobody seemed to know what made her son anxious. She felt that nobody understood her son as well as she did. I told her that this was undoubtedly true, and acted as a moderator for three prearranged phone calls so she could use her knowledge of Darrell to help staff understand why the calls led to such heated and at times abusive exchanges.

Darrell exhibited a high degree of physical agitation before, during, and after phone calls. Although they spoke every other day, the timing was haphazard. When he called her, Darrell often got the answering machine with a message delaying or postponing the call to the next day, which Darrell simply could not cope with. I eventually had a long talk about autism with Darrell's parents, explaining Darrell's need for regularity and predictability, and formulated three communication guidelines.

The first was to limit phone calls to two times per week: one initiated by the family, and one by Darrell. These calls would be at a fixed time with little or no variance. It was necessary to decrease the frequency of communication in order to decrease enmeshment, and it was necessary to have the predictability that Darrell needed to help him not be overwhelmed by anxiety.

The second communication guideline was that if Darrell became verbally abusive they were to tell him they could not continue speaking unless he was polite. If he continued to be insulting or unreasonable after *one prompt* they were to hang up. It had been my observation that Darrell could not hold positive feelings for long and I felt that it was better to terminate communication that only reinforced a negative internal state.

Looking at the family system as a whole, my third communication guideline for Darrell's parents was that they give Darrell clear messages and specific dates and times for all family visits, including those by his brother Michael. Darrell's ongoing litany of abuse regarding Michael's wife, Shirley, was Darrell's way of expressing his belief that she had taken his brother away from him. Thus it was especially important that there be no ambiguity about when he would see Darrell.

Although Darrell's parents were initially reluctant to accept these recommendations, I sensed a certain degree of relief. They eventually agreed to follow the communication guidelines and set consistent limits. I encouraged them to visit together (it was a three-hour drive) rather than separately, as a way of fostering the possibility of growth or healing in their relationship. It was also agreed that the moment Darrell began to be aggressive toward his mother she would withdraw. If Darrell wanted to go on an outing and get the things he wanted he would go with his father, with whom he generally had fewer behavioral problems. Darrell's parents soon began spending the night in town, thus having some time for themselves. They could also come back briefly the next day if the initial visit did not go well. Soon the anxious, compulsive, and ritualistic quality that characterized communication and contact between Darrell and his family was replaced by a more time-limited, structured, and happy way of being together.

Then, just when I thought I was out of the woods and in the clearing, everything seemed to fall apart. Darrell suddenly began refusing to go to school, spitting at others, throwing cups, and completely disrupting every environment he was in. I had come to consider myself well inoculated to Darrell's question-and-answer routine, but was quite taken aback one day when he said to me in a soft voice: "What would happen to me if I *raped my mother?*"

I finally realized that Darrell's perseverative speech at this time was largely focused on the dates and duration of his pending home visit for a family reunion. Everyone in Darrell's family was active in state politics and, in spite of their best intentions, the date of the family reunion kept changing due to the pressures of a current election.

I arranged a family meeting with Darrell's parents and his brother Michael and his wife Shirley. It became clear that, although they all felt committed to this family gathering, it was difficult to arrange a time that worked for everyone. There was an undercurrent of ambiguity that made me think they had mixed feelings about this plan. However, they came to understand the need for clarity and firmness of intent for Darrell's sake.

I invited Darrell to joined us and we went around the room with everyone present confirming the date and time of the upcoming family get-together. He was promised that it would not be changed. Darrell directed a few threatening gestures and obscene remarks toward Shirley, but was for the most part fairly well behaved. It was also made clear to Darrell that should he hit anyone or destroy property at home, he would be brought back to the group home immediately. The group home supervisor affirmed that staff would be assigned to make the drive and bring him back if that was necessary. Thus there was clarity about time, as well as behavioral limits and expectations. However, the visit was not contingent on behavior prior to departure, and it was also made clear to Darrell that if he felt anxious at any time before the visit he could choose not to go. In this way we avoided the "pressure cooker" situation of the past wherein Darrell's visits were contingent upon good behavior prior to leaving. This had created an all-or-nothing situation that he could not tolerate, which he responded to by acting out and preventing the visit.

This time Darrell did go home and, for the first time in many years, had a successful two-day visit without property destruction or aggression. The family wisely did not try to extend the visit, and drove him back as a group to his residence.

Darrell's relationships with group home staff members improved greatly as well. I came to be deeply impressed by the tolerance and graciousness of many of these young people who had worked with Darrell through very hard times. Although the structural systems approach did not address Darrell's behavior directly, he was no longer aggressive and they were appreciative of this.

Darrell now lives in a supported living environment close to his parents, who are very proud of him. They deserve a great deal of credit not only for their dedication to their son, but also for the courage to change family dynamics that ultimately facilitated Darrell's progress toward a better life. Figure 4–1 summarizes what was done in structural terms.

Figure 4–1

STRUCTURAL FAMILY SYSTEM SUMMARY

1. Shift focus from Darrell as identified patient to the family and care provider systems.
2. Regulate and facilitate clear communication.
3. Strengthen the executive subsystem (parental coalition).
4. Create clear boundaries between the family and care provider sybsystems.
5. Decrease mother–son enmeshment.
6. Strengthen father–son alliance.
7. Create interventions for anxiety at a systemic rather than a personal level.

5

EMERGING FROM THE AUTISTIC SHELL:

Psychodynamic Understanding and Discrete Trial Learning Help an Autistic Boy Develop His First Friendships

When Stuart's parents brought him for an assessment at the Stanton Program, I remember being struck by how, with his stylishly cut jet black hair, khaki slacks, and white dress shirt, he did not seem to be a child with a disability but rather a handsome, terribly shy young man. He was continually trying to hide behind his mother or slide under the table.

Stuart was 14 years of age and had been **autistic** from birth. As an infant, he had never cuddled normally, even while breastfeeding. His parents and teachers alike noted that he always seemed to be in a state of intense hyperarousal or anxiety. His only relief from this intense state seemed to come when he could sit alone in a quiet place, rocking silently or playing with his own or his father's dress shirts. He would tie the ends of the sleeves into strange balls of knots and then swing the two sleeves in opposite directions in an unusual and skillful way that I have only seen approximated by Alaskan natives, who use a unique kind of Eskimo yo-yo made of string and weighted fur pouches.

Although Stuart was able to say a large variety of words, he spoke in a very faint voice, and he resisted speaking when possible. One of his parents' goals regarding his coming to live at this six-bed group home was that he receive more intensive and consistent speech therapy. I learned that, while Stuart did have a positive attachment to his parents, he had never developed any friendships with peers and had a very difficult time with teachers in a variety of classroom settings. So another treatment goal that they had for him was to develop more positive relationships with others. Stuart was accepted into the Stanton Program. On his first day there, he refused to leave his bedroom. He simply sat near the clothes and toys that his parents had brought for him and refused to move. He kept taking his dress shirts from his closet and tying knots in the sleeves.

On his second day, the staff were unable to find him and had to begin an all-out search. After searching the house and surrounding area, they called the local police, who also kept an eye out for him as the program staff continued to wander local streets looking for this small, dark-haired autistic boy. After a few hours of searching, one tired staff member returned to Stuart's room and noticed something unusual in the placement of the furniture. The bed seemed to have been moved just a few inches further from the wall than usual. She pulled the blanket from the bed and discovered that the area between the bed and the wall seemed to be stuffed with shirts, underwear, and blue jeans. She pulled away a number of these clothing items only to find Stuart laying there, wedged between the bed and the wall, surrounded by a pile of his own clothing.

Over the following weeks, Stuart was quite resourceful in finding quiet places where he would not be disturbed. Staff repeatedly had to search for him, and they would inevitably find him rocking quietly in a peer's closet or sitting in a corner behind a desk or dresser, holding a shirt.

After about three weeks, he did begin developing tentative relationships with a few caregivers who had spent much of these early weeks with him. At times, he seemed to very much like having these staff sit quietly with him or join in his unique style of play with dress shirts. Also, he gradually did begin taking part in some activities with peers, though engaging him in conversation continued to be a challenge.

On one particularly hot day that summer, I went to see if Stuart might want to join his peers on an outing to a swimming pool. I found him sitting on his bed with three knotted dress shirts piled on his lap. I said, "Hi, Stuart. Would you like to go swimming today?"

"Tie," answered Stuart, as he began rocking.

"Do you want to go to the pool?"

He just continued rocking silently. I asked the question again, moving into his line of vision and gesturing gently as though I were swimming.

"Tie," said Stuart, as the intensity of his rocking increased slightly.

"What's that, Stuart?"

"Tie."

I said, "Oh, yes, you tied the shirt. Do you want to show me?" He simply turned away and continued rocking. I said, "Stuart, what would you like to do today?"

"Tie the shirt."

Everyone working with Stuart naturally wanted him to increase his engagement with others while decreasing his **self-stimulatory behaviors** such as his rocking and his perseverative play with dress shirts. From the point of view of caregivers, it often seems as if the person with autism lives behind a nearly impenetrable wall of isolation. Of course, the name autism itself implies that autistics live (to varying degrees) in worlds of their own, disconnected from shared social realities. As caregivers try to draw the autistic child into the world of interpersonal communication, they will often find themselves frustrated by the child's remarkable ability to become and remain wholly engrossed in self-stimulatory behaviors, blocking out all attempts to break through these barriers. Those new to working with people with autistic disorders have expressed surprise at finding that an autistic child will consistently seem to prefer repetitive, self-stimulatory play even when activities that most children find enjoyable are offered.

Because of the part that they seem to play in the autistic child's isolation, self-stimulatory behaviors are often seen as the enemy by those attempting to care for or educate the child with autism. However, direct attempts to take away or decrease these behaviors can often lead to increased anxiety, to the emergence of alternative avoidant behaviors, or even to fits of aggressive or **self-injurious**

behaviors. For these reasons, we have found that understanding the important functions that these behaviors serve for the child is essential to effectively helping the child.

First, it is important to note that we all engage in some self-stimulatory behaviors. During a long lecture or business meeting, one will find people doodling, twirling their hair, tapping their fingers, or chewing on a pen. We generally engage in these behaviors unconsciously for any of a number of reasons. Most often, though, they seem to provide a sort of relief or mental escape from mildly unpleasant situations. Of course, one does not literally escape, but these behaviors may provide a somewhat soothing physical sensation that distracts us from our surroundings.

In many cases, individuals with autism are experts at escaping by distracting themselves using simple physical sensations. In Stuart's case, we sometimes noted that he did not seem to hear or see things going on around him when he was engrossed or absorbed in his rocking and the swinging of dress shirt sleeves. On one occasion, I noted that when his parents arrived for a visit and Stuart was in his room rocking, he did not seem to see them as they were walking in his door. Even as they walked up to him and enthusiastically greeted him, waving and smiling, there was no reaction at all, so that one would almost have suspected that he was blind. But then, when his mother put her hand on his shoulder, Stuart jerked as if a spell had been broken. He seemed utterly startled to see his mother and began shouting "Mommy, Mommy, Mommy," for a few moments as he gradually calmed down.

Frances Tustin (1980, 1984, 1986, 1988, 1990), a leading object relations analyst from England who has worked for many years with autistic children, has written extensively on how these children use auto-generated sensations to block out frightening intrusions from the outside world. Her conclusions are based on years of observation and therapy with young children with autism. She describes how these children create a **protective shell** or **autistic encapsulation** made up of self-stimulated sensations that "serves a useful purpose as a refuge from unbearable, seemingly life-threatening experiences" (Tustin 1990).

No one is certain why people with autism perceive many ordinary interpersonal reactions as confusing and terrifying, but the observation that they do perceive them this way is not unique to Tustin. Temple Grandin (1995), one well-known, very highly accomplished woman with autism, once described her own experience as follows: "I recognized that fear was my great motivator. . . . At that time I didn't realize that other people experience other major emotions" (p. 94). Donna Williams (1992), another highly successful autistic woman, wrote that she lived in an "emotionless and empty shell" (p. 56) which served to block out overwhelming feelings of terror.

In our work with Stuart, it became clear that his avoidant and self-stimulatory behaviors were largely a function of intense fears that venturing into new activities or engaging in highly stimulating interpersonal interactions would overwhelm or even destroy him. Stuart's perceptions and emotions seemed to be much more finely tuned than those of a normal child, so that loud noises or unexpected changes would send him running or cause him to "disappear" into the sensations of his rocking. So we recognized that trying to force him to interact or to come out of his protective shell would not be effective.

We decided to use a "Turtle Program" with Stuart—a creative intervention integrating the understanding discussed above with the practicality of **discrete trial learning** that a young, very empathic professional in the field named Nicole Robbins had helped to create. When frightened, turtles naturally retreat into their shells. In such circumstances, one cannot force the turtle to come out. However, if one creates an environment of safety and is patient, one can certainly succeed in enticing a turtle to come out and look around. The Turtle Program used this metaphor to help the staff and Stuart himself to understand the most effective way of helping him to increase his engagement in social interactions.

The program began simply (see Figure 5–1). When Stuart was feeling overwhelmed, he would be allowed to go to the safety of his room to play with his dress shirts. Twice per day during a quiet time of the day, a staff would approach him and say that it was time for his Turtle Program. If he was willing to pause from self-stimulation to answer two questions about how his day had been, how he was

The Turtle Program

Date: _____

Two times per day, during a relaxing, quiet time, ask Stuart to *come out of his shell*. On each of these two occasions, the goal is for Stuart to pause from any self-stimulatory behaviors, attend to staff, and answer *two questions*. (Questions can be on how he's feeling, what he's done today, what he wants to do later, etc.)

If Stuart answers both questions, he immediately receives a favorite snack (green olives, graham crackers, or yogurt).

Trial #1:

Question 1: _____

Answered: Yes   No

Question 2: _____

Answered: Yes   No

Reward: _____

Trial #2:

Question 1: _____

Answered: Yes   No

Question 2: _____

Answered: Yes   No

Reward: _____

Figure 5–1

feeling, or what he wanted to do later on, then he would immediately receive a favorite snack—either green olives with red pimentos, yogurt, or graham crackers. We already knew that he was easily capable of answering two such questions. Our idea at this point was not to demand something new but rather to help him develop a feeling of comfort and regularity regarding these interactions.

Because success was easy for Stuart, he began enjoying these Turtle Program interactions, and so, after a few weeks, we increased the criteria for success slightly so that Stuart would not only answer two questions but also ask one. A couple of weeks later, he had to ask two questions. Within a few of months, Stuart had become quite accustomed to having relaxed conversations with his caregivers during a couple of quiet times during the day, and the interactions began to seem quite natural.

At this point, we continued what we had been doing but also added the expectation that once per day Stuart would choose a peer, approach him, and make at least one very brief statement or ask one brief question of him. Over the next few months, as Stuart's comfort with others increased, we were able to increase the range of rewards he could be given for success. He began regularly going on drives to see the horses at a local stable, going to the Jacuzzi, and even going to the swimming pool as a reward.

Most important of all, through these regular, structured interactions, Stuart began developing real relationships. He started more freely expressing his actual likes and dislikes during and outside of these sessions. Also, when he was asked to approach a peer to converse, he often chose the same couple of peers. Soon, he began to approach and interact with them spontaneously and even playfully at times other than those prescribed by the program.

Clearly, Stuart is still autistic. When there is a lot going on around him, he still becomes overstimulated, retreating into his own world. Also, he does not often understand the subtler aspects of social interactions and is not capable of the independence of his nondisabled teenage peers.

However, his quality of life has improved greatly and he has developed his first friendships. During a recent visit, Stuart's parents were very surprised when they went to Stuart's room and did not find him there. They went out into the back yard and found Stuart standing on the grass beside the swing set with a friend of his who was also a young man with autism. Stuart was swinging the sleeves of a dress shirt in the unique way he had for many years. His friend was also holding a dress shirt, unsuccessfully trying to make the knotted sleeves swing in harmony as Stuart was. When Stuart noticed the difficulty that his friend was having, they looked at each other, and they both laughed.

6

MOURNING WHAT IS GONE:

A Psychodynamic Approach with an Autistic Patient

Frances Tustin's (1980, 1984, 1986, 1990) in-depth description of how children with autism use auto-generated, physical sensations to create a **protective shell**, blocking out terrifying or overwhelming aspects of the world, has proven very helpful in my own work with autistic children and young adults. Tustin (1988) also wrote extensively about doing object relations psychotherapy with autistic children, which I initially found less relevant for the following reason.

In North America today, the treatment of autism relies almost exclusively on behavioral, educational, and psychopharmacological interventions. Psychotherapy—particularly psychodynamic psychotherapy—is seen as irrelevant. Because Bettelheim's (1967) theory of the "refrigerator mother" (that children become autistic due to unloving, threatening mothers) caused so much guilt and pain for families of autistic children just a few decades ago, there is a reasonable sense of mistrust toward psychodynamic psychotherapy on the part of many families and professionals involved with autism. Having been deeply influenced by this climate of opinion, in spite of my training in object relations, I came to rely on cognitive and behavioral approaches in my work with autistic children and adolescents. However, my experiences with an autistic client named Paul changed my views on this subject in a significant way.

Paul was a tall, blond 22-year-old with autism. He had never been very interested in social activities. However, over the past year, his parents had become quite concerned about his increased unwilling-ness to leave the house and had asked me to see him for individual psychotherapy. Paul had limited expressive speech that often showed **echolalia**. Over recent months, he had become extremely **persevera-tive**, often talking for hours on end about his father when he was away at work or about the whereabouts of the family station wagon. When anyone tried to get him to stop or to engage his attention elsewhere, he often became extremely agitated, sometimes jumping up and biting, pinching, or hitting the person nearest to him.

A wide range of behavioral and cognitive techniques had been tried to modify Paul's behaviors, but his condition had continued to worsen. His parents had consulted a psychiatrist with extensive experience in this field. Based on his belief that Paul was depressed, the psychiatrist had recently prescribed an antidepressant medication.

I was initially hesitant to begin psychotherapy with Paul because of his limited language skills, serious aggressive behaviors, and history of poor response to cognitive-behavioral interventions. It was due largely to the encouragement of Paul's psychiatrist, whose opinion I re-spected, that I took the case on.

Our initial sessions were quite challenging. Often, Paul would come into my office and ask a question such as, "Where's the car?"

I might respond with, "What car is that, Paul?"

He would inevitably answer, "Where's the car?"

I might next respond with, "Well, my car is outside."

He would then say, "Outside. My car is outside." Paul often confused pronouns, saying "my" for "your" or "yours" for "mine." He would then again ask, "Where's the car?" Such perseverative exchanges might continue for up to 20 or 30 minutes. Attempts to change the subject usually failed. If I ignored his questions, he often would become highly agitated and, on one occasion, he grabbed me, digging his nails into my arm.

On some occasions, we had perplexing exchanges during which Paul would talk about something that was "gone" or "broken." For example, one day he suddenly blurted out, "It's gone!"

I asked, "What is gone?"

He said, "What *is* gone!"

I then said, "Can you tell me what's gone or where it went?"

He then began repeating the word "gone" in a mournful tone.

Over my first few months of 40-minute sessions with Paul, I tried introducing him to art therapy involving paints, markers, and clay. I also tried play therapy using a sandtray, but he showed no interest in these activities. He wanted to either rock silently in my office or engage in perseverative exchanges like the one described above.

On the positive side, I did feel that a rapport was developing between us, and his parents reported that coming to my office was one of the only things that got Paul to voluntarily leave the house. So I decided that rather than trying to get Paul to engage in specific activities that did not interest him, I would focus on being *empathically present* with him and on *understanding* the *meaning* the perseverative exchanges that he engaged in held for him.

During this period, I also referred back to some of Tustin's writings on therapy with autistic individuals. I was heartened by her advice (1992) that "We need to wait patiently for the appropriate moments when we can demonstrate" to the autistic individual that "human beings, in spite of their unpredictability and mortality, give more long-term and effective support" than the protective, autistic shell on which they so heavily rely (p. 122).

It seemed to me that not only was Paul's rocking part of his personal way of creating sensations to block out shared social realities, but that his perseverative exchanges, though ostensibly interactive, actually served as a way of avoiding more genuine, spontaneous conversation. In this regard, I also kept in mind Tustin's (1980) warning that if a therapist allows the autistic individual to use their interactions as part of his typical autistic style of behavior then "we leave him in the grip of his pathology with no possibility for developing genuine relationships characterized by effort and coopera-tion" (p. 33).

What really struck me in a powerful way, though, was Tustin's observation that when a number of the young, autistic children she worked with began tentatively moving out of the sensation-dominated world of autistic encapsulation, they would begin mourning the loss of this unusual, yet safe and familiar world. She noted (1988) that such children would "often say 'gone' very mournfully" (p. 97) and that for some previously mute children, *gone* and *broken* were often their first words. I was quite surprised that a therapist on the other side of the globe, working with young, British autistic children had had experiences so similar to my own experiences with Paul. Tustin held that it was the therapist's job to help autistic children who had reached this point through the process of *mourning* the loss of their old way of being. She also stressed the importance of encouraging them to connect with others. While I felt that these goals might be relevant with Paul, I was also conscious that he was much older than Tustin's patients, and so it would be important to encourage development without pushing him beyond what he was ready to deal with.

During our actual sessions, I focused on neither rejecting nor indulging Paul's perseverative speech. I engaged in enough repetitive exchanges with him to prevent him from becoming so overanxious that he would retreat into self-stimulatory rocking, and I demanded that he talk about subjects other than those he typically perseverated on. I also began talking with Paul about what I believed the underlying *meaning* of his perseverations might be, rather than repeatedly giving the set responses that he had come to expect to his questions.

For example, one day he was perseverating on the family station wagon in which his mother had driven him to my office: "Sitting in the *seat*. Seat, seat. Where's the wagon? Seat is *gone*. Gone, gone, gone. . . . Where's the wagon?"

Instead of answering his question, I replied, "It sounds like you miss being in the station wagon. I think you miss the *feeling*—being in the *seat*. Do you also miss your mom?"

Paul then became quiet for almost two minutes. Then he said, "Miss . . . seat. *Seat* is *gone*."

Although a nonautistic person would have associated the drive with the wagon as a whole and, perhaps, with the person in the wagon with him, because Paul was so absorbed in momentary sensations, the word *seat* best captured his experience of driving with his mother.

I replied, "Yes. The seat is gone right now. It's not here."

He then replied, "It's gone," and was able to move on to other topics.

Donna Williams (1992), a very high-functioning autistic writer, has discussed how she was always "talking via objects" (p. 167) so that her language was not understood by those around her; it was a language of idiosyncratic symbolism that she herself describes as "evasive jargon" and complex "poetrylike speech" (p. 167). Tustin (1988) notes that the therapist must enter and understand the child's world without allowing himself to become "null and void" (p. 100), being lulled into an autistic-like state himself.

In my own experience with Paul, as I strove to understand the meanings of his perseverative speech, I often found it quite challenging to keep myself from allowing the repetitive nature of his perseverations to lull me into an almost trancelike or sleeplike state. Since my work with Paul, I have come to think of psychotherapy with autistic clients as a long, gentle *battle* to bring thought, contact, and language to the empty spaces of the mind.

An interesting and significant period of my work with Paul began when he began perseverating about a door that was broken. At the end of the session, I asked his mother if she knew what door he might be speaking of, and she said that she wasn't aware of any broken doors in the house. The next session, Paul came in and immediately began by saying, "Where's the door? It's *broken. Broken, broken, broke- broke-broke- broken.* Where's the door?"

I simply replied, "I don't know, Paul. Where is the broken door?"

He then said, "Where's the door? It's broken. Turn the knob. It's *broken, broken, broke- bro- bro- bro- bro- broken. Broken.* Where's the door?"

I then said, "The door—is it out there or in your mind?" I wasn't sure at all that he would understand what I meant by "in your mind." Paul became silent. What was unusual about this silence was that he did not begin rocking. He leaned forward and sat very still as if he were deep in thought. I decided to remain silent with him, waiting. Paul did not move or say a word for nearly fifteen minutes. I struggled to stay empathically present in the warm, still air of the office. Then Paul turned and made eye contact. Many people with autism have difficulty making eye contact, and Paul very rarely did so unless someone actively demanded it of him. In a quiet voice, Paul said, "In your *mind*. It's in your mind." Then he began rocking.

Though he had again confused his pronouns, the manner in which Paul made this statement certainly made me consider the possibility that he was developing a new level of self-awareness. Over the next few weeks, he became increasingly capable of explaining whether something he was talking about was an external object or inner thought/memory about a *sensation-object*. This was very difficult for Paul, as his awareness had generally been so dominated by immediate sensations. For Paul, things were either here or they were *gone*—as in nonexistent; they could be used for sensory self-stimulation or they were *broken*. I was working with Paul on understanding that something could be physically gone while still being present in his thoughts—in his mind. When one is within the protective autistic shell, one is in a state akin to sleep or daydreaming; Donna Williams (1992) referred to it as being a "nobody, nowhere" (p. xiii). Paul's awareness that things could be "gone" or "broken" was a like a crack in this autistic shell. It led to confusion and even terror on his part. His protective shell of self-stimulatory sensations had been like a dreamy, protective mother to Paul, blocking out confusing, overstimulating, and unpredictable input from the outside world. Becoming genuinely aware of the existence of outer and inner worlds, of social realities, and of the painful process of change meant losing the dreamy mother, the predictable noplace that he had lived in nearly all of his life. Paul was not sure that he wanted to walk through that "door," which was broken and was breaking his autistic shell; it was understandable that he felt deep grief, ambivalence, and confusion about such a process of growth.

Many of these issues came up clearly in a session a few weeks later. Paul came in again saying, "Where's the wagon? It's gone. Where's the wagon?"

I said, "Well, you know that your mom just left in her station wagon. So you must be talking about another wagon."

He said, "It's gone. The wagon is gone." Then he paused, looked at me, and said, "Hi. Nice day."

I said, "Yes. It is."

A few minutes after he let go of his perseveration on the wagon being "gone," though, he began repeating that something was "broken." I asked whether he was again talking about the door, but he did not respond. I made a few other guesses, but he did not stop perseverating until I asked him, "Paul, do you feel that mom is broken?"

He replied, "Not broken! *Broken. Broken, bro- bro- bro- broken, broken . . .*"

I then said, "Is Paul-Mommy-Daddy broken?"

Paul stopped his repetition and looked up. Then, for the first time since I'd known him, he began to cry. He sobbed quietly, as tears streamed down his face. He cried like this for the remaining twenty minutes of the session.

When his mother arrived to pick him up, Paul stopped crying and walked to meet her. "Hello, Mom. Ready to go."

His mother could see that he had been crying. She said, "He *never* cries."

From this point on, Paul's depression gradually lifted. He became increasingly interested in taking part in activities, and his parents found him a part-time job with a supported employment agency and enrolled him in a therapeutic day program.

Paul continued to rock and perseverate at times, but his parents were very happy with his willingness to be more active and with a noticeable decrease in the amount of time he spent engaged in self-stimulatory behavior. Within a year, his aggressive behaviors had almost entirely disappeared.

It is very well known that many people with autism have difficulty with transitions and change. However, through my work with Paul and with other autistic adolescents and adults, I have found that psychotherapy can sometimes turn an autistic's difficulty with change from an ordeal into an opportunity. By seeking the underlying functions or meanings of his perseverative speech and ritualized behaviors and by helping him to use language more effectively, to let go, and to mourn what is "gone," one can help a person with autism to open the door—even if only a little way—to new possiblities.

7

MIRRORED:

From Aggression
to a More Positive
Sense of Self

Sarah's diagnostic history was complex and convoluted. Her mother, an extremely bright and loving woman who had adopted Sarah at birth, had kept a bound file of all medical work-ups and medication trials. It was a daunting document. Sarah had been to two neuropsychiatric institutes and a long chain of pediatricians, neurologists, psychiatrists, psychologists, and other experts in the field of developmental disabilities. By the age of 13 she had been assigned just about every disorder of childhood in the *DSM-III* and **DSM-IV**. This diagnostic odyssey from one psychological assessment and professional opinion to another had been both mystifying and disheartening for Sarah's mother and father, who had done everything they possibly could for Sarah.

Sarah had come to our treatment center due to the sudden closing of her former residence—an all-too-common occurrence in the current climate of budget crunches and low rates for service providers. When I met Sarah during the initial evaluation she sat demurely with her head drooping. Her arms were heavily scarred with self-inflicted bite marks. She was making a big effort to "be good," looking at her mother anxiously before answering questions. She was stocky, with a broad face and large brown eyes. Beneath the subdued veneer I detected an undercurrent of willfulness and explosive energy. This manifested slightly when we started talking about animals. Her head came up at once, her eyes wide and expressive as she told me about where grizzly bears and tigers lived and how they killed their prey. Sarah intrigued me from the moment I met her, and I quickly filed her history of aggression in a remote corner of my mind, hoping that she would improve in a more structured environment and bring a painful journey to a happy end.

Oddly enough, this clinical fantasy was reinforced during the initial month of Sarah's stay. She was quiet, compliant, and seemed to be a model student. I saw her once a week and had her write in a special book about difficult feelings and situations with the other residents in her new home. But just when it seemed that a remarkable transformation had taken place, Sarah started biting smaller children and attacking staff. When demands were placed on her at school she started screaming, creating chaos in the classroom. I began to get emergency calls from her teacher every other day. The residential staff said she was creating an unsafe environment by victimizing younger peers, biting, pulling hair, and at times injuring herself. She was becoming a danger to self and others, and rapidly approaching discharge criteria. Honeymoon over.

Sarah now refused to write or talk in our weekly meetings. She sat with arms folded, pouting. She would scream when any request to communicate was made. She also had a pat explanation for her behavior, which she delivered in a pressured, angry manner.

"It's not my fault. My birth parents had a drug and alcohol problem. They were very bad people. They were negligent. Because they did drugs and alcohol I got damaged. I got damaged by their bad habit of using drugs and alcohol. I was a drug and alcohol baby. I'm damaged. That's why I have a hard time. I can't help it. It's my birth parents' fault. People who have kids shouldn't abuse drugs and alcohol like my birth parents did. I'm really mad at them for doing that. They ruined my life. When I'm 18 I'll never drink alcohol. I'll drink nonalcoholic beer."

It was like a litany. Whenever I tried to discuss an incident that happened she would go on autopilot about her birth parents. She knew she had been adopted at birth and that her biological mother, whom she referred to as her "birth mother," had a drug and alcohol problem. Whenever I challenged her about her aggressive behavior she would stiffen her back, fold her hands on her chest, and say smugly, "Well . . . I have Fetal Alcohol Syndrome. I can't help it. It's not fair what my birth parents did. . . ."

Depending on my response, she would then up the ante by breaking into tears and screaming about how much she hated where she was and how badly she wanted to go home. If I tried to reason with her about moving on from the past to make her life better now she would scream even louder and tear up anything within reach. On one occasion she tore up the Ungame, beheaded a Pound Puppy, threw two Power Rangers out the window, and cleared my desk in the blink of an eye. When she consented to talk to me, she let her imagination run wild, jumping from one topic to another. She had a fascination with African animals killing their prey. She also talked at length about people who killed other people with knives or by setting them on fire, throwing acid in their face, or burying them alive.

The situation was further complicated by Sarah's overt sexuality and her history of being molested at a former placement. She would fondle herself publicly and talk about sex with anyone who passed by. While sitting quietly in class she would suddenly shout, "Penis! Penis!" She would tell the checkout clerk at the local pharmacy that she was having her period and had a vaginal rash. She was provocative with boys, and would then accuse them of being "inappropriate," reporting them regularly to staff. Her parents were extremely concerned about her safety in this regard, given that she was molested by staff at her former placement.

The problems were piling up and there were no obvious solutions. Sarah had initially responded to contingency contracts and hourly reinforcement schedules that allowed her to earn candy or sodas for the absence of aggression. But now she simply didn't care, and everyone was at their wit's end. There were two distinct faces Sarah had shown us. The one she was currently displaying I called Sarah the Destroyer. But not entirely overshadowed and in dire need of support was an extremely bright, entertaining girl with wants, needs, and dreams.

Upon deeper reflection I concluded that we had become so involved with external behavior that we were not attending to the individual behind the behavior, which is to say we were neglecting relevant aspects of Sarah's inner self. When she was screaming, all we could think of was how to get her to stop. We were not listening to what she was screaming *for*.

I began to pay more attention to what Sarah was screaming about. And, of course, she capitalized on this. The drill was as follows. She would start screaming in the classroom to avoid a demand. She would get placed outside and continue screaming until the teacher called me. I would come over and promise her a soda if she would talk about what was upsetting her. She would stop at once, and off we went.

Seasoned staff who adhered to a strictly behavioral approach began to resent my role as they felt I was reinforcing her negative behavior. I got to come in as the good guy and spend time with the well-behaved Sarah while they struggled with a screaming biting Sarah all day long. I was clearly being manipulated, and no lasting good could come of what I was doing. In spite of these objections I continued to work with Sarah, although I did limit the emergency sessions to one per week.

A theme soon emerged in sessions in regard to Sarah's "automatic crying" about how badly she wanted to go home. Most children in residential treatment programs want to go back home if they have any kind of a home. Over time, there is a tendency to become desensitized to this issue. In Sarah's case, she had routinely complained about being at a place with "retarded" kids, but nobody paid much attention to this. She often said she wanted to go to a "normal" school and live like children who had regular lives. I thought that there was a message here that we had missed.

When possible, I began to openly discuss behavioral reports with Sarah. When I asked her about interpersonal conflicts she would say with great indignation: "Well . . . he was *looking at me!* It made me feel bad . . . real bad." Sarah couldn't explain why looking at her made her angry, but I hypothesized that there was an underlying problem involving mirroring.

It has to be understood that in the field of developmental disabilities it is almost taboo to think in terms of self psychology when "the empirical research" indicates a behavioral approach is what works. However, in Sarah's case behavioral approaches were *not* working. A number of medication changes to prevent the issuance of a 72-hour discharge had also been ineffective.

Sarah's intense dislike for a boy with Down's Syndrome, who often "looked at" her, revealed something of how her negative sense of self was triggered by peers she perceived as defective or weak. Due to this boy's different physical appearance, Sarah called him "retarded" and became upset whenever he came into visual range. It was also significant that Sarah attacked peers she perceived as weak. I reasoned that Sarah was angry about feelings of weakness and defectiveness in herself. She felt that she was somehow a mistake, an accident, the result of bad choices by her biological parents, and so she attacked outside herself what she could not process or tolerate inside herself. Hence her repeated claim that "I'm not a bad person. It's not my fault," as well as her ritualistic blame of her biological parents.

Sarah's tangential thought processes made it difficult to piece things together, but she often referred to an older girl in another program who she thought was "really pretty," and said she wanted to be "just like Suzie." She had had no contact with Suzie, but had developed a strong *idealization*. When she spoke about Suzie, she became noticeably calmer. This led me to think that if Sarah was in an environment she perceived as more "normal" with adolescents she could idealize, she might benefit from mirroring through a **twinship bond** (Kohut 1984) with peers she admired. Both Kohut and Mahler (Kramer and Akhtar 1994) believed that mirroring has two important functions in the development of a strong and healthy self:

1. Positive mirroring helps to define and establish a *cohesive* self. When you are mirrored through eye contact and other reciprocal interactions with a positive figure, a positive sense of self gets built up that holds together under stress.

2. Positive mirroring confirms and regulates self-esteem. You get to feel good about yourself when mirrored by a positive or admired other. Continued positive mirroring sustains self-esteem.

I began to see that embedded in Sarah's oppositional-defiant behavior and tantrums were screaming *self-statements* that just weren't being heard.

Most group homes and treatment centers have behavioral criteria for admission to the programs they offer. Children and adolescents who demonstrate improved behavior move to what is often referred to as *less restrictive* programs. When mental and behavioral decompensation occurs, the move is toward a more restrictive program. And so, when I recommended that Sarah be transferred to a program with older and more socially mature girls, my request was not taken seriously.

Fortunately, Amie, the supervisor of the program I had in mind, was in the process of getting her master's degree in clinical psychology and was willing to listen to my rationale. I told her that she and her staff would have to feel **empathy** to Sarah, and be ready to tolerate some very bizarre behavior at the start.

I explained to Amie that Sarah's parents had both been very loving and attentive to her through early childhood, but that her neurological condition seemed to have resulted in a definite developmental arrest in the areas of communication, empathy, and reciprocal relationships. She was moderately mentally retarded, and yet she had an acute social awareness in regard to levels of authority and social hierarchies at school. Sarah suffered more than we knew, I explained, because she had severe cognitive and emotional limitations, yet she was at times acutely aware of these limitations.

To make my point with Amie, I gave her some details about my therapy sessions with Sarah. I would sit with Sarah and let her scream at the top her lungs for half an hour. Often three or four people would come to my door to ask if I needed help. I did this because Sarah was not only venting her frustration and anger about certain people, but was also grieving aloud about what it was like to be trapped inside a disabled brain. Sarah could identify with other children who did not suffer her limitations. She wanted to be just like them but couldn't. However, if she had an opportunity *live* with adolescents who would give her positive mirroring, this might give her a more positive sense of self and decrease her problematic behavior.

When Amie discussed this with her staff, an objection was raised that warranted consideration. Sarah had a tic, and there was a concern that if the older, street-smart girls saw Sarah repeatedly biting her arm they might make fun of her, which could be devastating to her self-esteem. However, it was my belief that Sarah, being younger and lower-functioning, was not threatening to the older girls. There was also the possibility that they would mentor Sarah like a younger sister. The staff eventually agreed that, if they could encourage the other girls to take on a helping role, this would be good for them and Sarah alike.

So Sarah moved. She was very insecure in the beginning, but the incidents of aggression decreased immediately. Due to her desire to fit in and be accepted by those she looked up to, she did not act out and draw negative attention to herself. When there was adequate evidence that the change would work, Sarah became Suzie's roommate, which gave her what could be called an *idealizing self-object experience*, which has been defined as "a need to experience oneself as being part of an admired and respected selfobject other; a need for the opportunity to be accepted by, and merge into, a . . . protective other who possesses qualities the subject experiences as lacking in the self" (Kramer and Akhtar, p. 73).

What needs to be emphasized in this case is the fact that once the treatment focus shifted from behavior management to the issues of self-identity and self-esteem, a solution was found that eventually led to a dramatic decrease in aggressive behavior. The point being made here is that when behavioral treatment fails, try something else. We provided as many opportunities as we could for Sarah to feel good about herself. We arranged for weekly visits by a "big sister" from a nearby college. Sarah often spoke about how she was going to be "just like" her. A colleague of mine who ran a substance abuse program invited Sarah to participate in a group with expectant mothers. This gave Sarah a way of processing her anger toward her biological mother in a more positive way. Sarah was very proud that she had been able to "prevent more fetal alcohol babies from being born."

As Sarah developed a more positive sense of self, her oppositional-defiant behavior decreased significantly. There was ongoing concern for some time that she would copy the delinquent behavior of some of the older girls, but this did not happen. Sarah preferred to associate with quieter girls who were either attractive or had a skill she admired.

Two years later, Sarah still speaks at length about her drug-and alcohol-abusing birth parents to anyone who will lend an ear. And she is still very sensitive about being called names. However, she has learned to cope with what she calls the "bad thoughts" that upset her. She has learned positive self-talk, such as "I'm okay just the way I am," and "Everyone has problems sometimes," which calms her down when she becomes upset.

At age 15 Sarah still finds herself going through internal struggles about whether she is a "little girl" or "big girl," but she has continued to move on to more independent living environments. Fortunately, there are always older girls she looks up to who accept her, take her under their wing, and in so doing help her sustain a more coherent and positive sense of self.

8

THE ORDER OF
THE FIST AND
THE HAND:

Imagery-Based
Character Education
as a Replacement for
Gang Identification

On one of my first visits to the Oakwood House, I noticed Luis talking with one of the staff about how he had been good and deserved to join in on an outing to the beach. With one hand, he was tugging on the staff member's sleeve as he spoke. His other hand was behind his back; with it, he was giving his peer, Scotty, "the finger."

Scotty quickly walked over and slapped Luis on the head. Luis shouted to the staff, "Hey, you saw that! I didn't do nothing! I was just here talking with you. Scotty shouldn't get to go if I don't!"

There were fourteen young men, aged 14 to 19, living at the Oakwood House. All of the residents had some form of developmental disability, Mild Mental Retardation being the most common diagnosis. Many had at least one additional diagnosis ranging from ADHD to Conduct Disorder. Almost all of them had been neglected or abused in some way. I had been asked to consult on the therapeutic milieu because of steadily escalating behavioral problems. For example, during the week prior to my being called, a group of clients had gone AWOL overnight and there had been eleven fistfights.

Although the Oakwood House was located in a relatively quiet, suburban area, as one went inside the house it often felt as if one were entering a very different reality. These young men were from some of the most violent neighborhoods of Los Angeles and San Francisco. And, as they say, though they had taken the boys out of the neighborhood, they hadn't taken the neighborhood out of the boys. They had clearly internalized the violent, tense atmosphere of their home communities, and it was palpable as one came into the living room of their large suburban home.

As I got to know the residents there, I learned that many of their behavioral problems resulted from ganglike behavior. In the absence of adequate parenting and positive role models, they had learned that the primary way to gain autonomy, status, and power was through affiliation with a gang. A few of the older residents had actually been in gangs, and all of them had wanted to. They had learned that it was essential to act tough and affiliate with other tough kids to survive.

Splits between the residents sometimes formed along racial lines. For example, one day during a basketball game, a resident of Mexican descent had said to an African-American resident, "Shit, you can't play. I thought that you n_____ knew how to shoot hoops." Without hesitation, the African-American resident threw the ball at his peer's head, leading to a fight involving six clients. Even after such an incident was over, the tension between the clients involved would remain, often leading to further incidents over the following weeks.

The residents were also very sensitive about their disabilities, and they often used their tough banter to mask them. However, a question involving any complex cognitive processing or requiring an answer outside of their scripted, "gangsta" banter quickly revealed that they could not process information easily. Although the residents were often patient with each other's disabilities, when someone did insult a peer's mental ability the reaction was usually violent. For example, one day I saw a staff member trying to get two clients to resolve a problem peacefully. He said, "Peter, I want you to listen to what Jamal is saying, okay?" Peter replied, "I ain't gonna listen to that retard!" A few seconds later, the staff and I were trying to separate the two of them who were on the ground, with punches flying.

After spending a few weeks observing and taking part in activities around the program, a number of observations had crystallized. First, these young men desperately needed *positive role models*. When I asked what he most needed to improve, one resident had replied, "I don't got no one to look up to, man. These staff here are all right, but they just leave after a while." Another observation was that the staff themselves needed more *structure* to facilitate *learning* and genuine *communication*. Often the staff would attempt to be caring and empathic, only to find the residents getting out of control; at other times, they would provide strict structure, and the clients would become quiet, compliant, and attentive. It also struck me very powerfully that these young men needed something positive to identify with as a replacement for the gang identity which they held onto so rigidly.

Around this time, I became aware of the Character Counts program, which was developed by the Josephson Institute for Ethics. I learned about it from the Devereux School in Glenholme, CT, which had had great success in combating "violence, incivility, irresponsibility, and dishonesty by strengthening the moral fiber of the next generation" (Megan 1996). This program attempts to influence kids' ways of thinking, feeling, and behaving using a milieu and, ultimately, a community approach. Many exercises and activities are used to teach children about the "Six Pillars of Character." These are trustworthiness, respect for others, responsibility, fairness, caring, and citizenship. One of the goals of the program was "to make the six pillars of character 'cool'" to kids (Maker 1996).

Given the success that numerous schools and communities had had with this program, and given its relevance to the needs of the residents of Oakwood House, I felt that its implementation there would be beneficial. In talking with the staff of the program, though, they felt that the house also needed a single *image* that could serve to unify the kids' vision of what they were working on. They wanted something that would excite and interest the kids. Also, we knew that memorizing the six pillars of character would be difficult for many of them, and we felt that an image could serve as a positive cue for the values and behaviors we were trying to encourage.

I have long been a believer in the power of images or myths to evoke new potentials. I was reminded of James Hillman's (1975) statement that "imagining things in a personal form" helps us "so that we can find access to them with our hearts" (p. 14). I was also reminded of Joseph Campbell's (1972) observation that "the imageries of mythology and religion serve positive, life-furthering ends," evoking "the wisdom of the species by which man has weathered the millenniums" (p. 13). In meeting and talking with the staff, we discussed many possible mythic images that we might use to help the residents of Oakwood House find access to the themes of the Character Counts program with their hearts.

Ultimately, we decided that the image of the knight—an image of masculine strength in the service of good—would capture the kids' imaginations. Working closely with an extremely imaginative and intelligent young professional named Kirk Hoffman, we developed a program called The Order of the Fist and the Hand (see Figure 8–1). We made it clear that each resident of the house had the potential to become a member of this order. However, to be a member they would have to understand and be committed to the Order's principles.

The Six Pillars of Character became the order's code, by which its members would strive to live. Each potential member also learned that the fist symbolized *self-control* and the hand symbolized *brotherhood*. The idea here was that the fist—formerly a symbol of fighting for these young men—would gradually be linked to anger management exercises. We often spoke with them about how real power comes when you can control yourself, and being a real man is proven through the fist of self-control, not through violence. And the theme of the hand as brotherhood was important in trying to develop a group identity that was inclusive of all house members, not one divided along racial or other lines. We explained to them that the handshake itself originated with the knights; they would hold out their open hands to each other as a way of showing that they were not holding a weapon with which they might attack. Similarly, these young men would need to hold out their hands to each other as "brothers," not holding tricks or insults behind their backs.

We held weekly group meetings to discuss specific themes related to the Pillars of Character. At times, we discussed the obstacles to brotherhood. We emphasized taking responsibility for one's own role in a problem by using "I" statements. For example, one day Luis was saying, "Man, Peter ain't no brother of mine. He was dissing me, and that's why I got in trouble. This is bull!" We could see Peter getting agitated. But by working with Luis we got him to a point where he could say, "Peter, listen, I feel pissed because I was really trying not to get in trouble. When you teased me and I lost it, that wrecked it for me. Man, don't do that no more, okay?"

Peter then said, "All right, Luis, all right," as he held out his hand. Luis gestured as if he was going to refuse Peter's handshake but then sighed, smiled, and shook his hand.

During our anger management classes, we also used a video series called BeCool, produced by the James Stanfield Company in Santa Barbara, California. This series presents videos designed to teach young people to face a variety of difficult situations appropriately. The repeated theme is to avoid a hot, angry response or a cold, passive response, striving for a *cool*, assertive response. We found this program quite helpful in setting up role plays and valuable discussions.

It is also worth noting that we did not limit the implementation of this program to specific group sessions. Laminated posters with the logo for the Order of the Fist and the Hand (Figure 8–1) and with the Six Pillars of Character (Figure 8–2) on them were posted around the house and in the residents' rooms. Also, homework assignments involving being caring or being a good citizen were given. For example, we would ask them to each do an act of kindness for someone else and report back on it the following week. Most of them clearly enjoyed the group. It was a place where there was enough structure for them to feel safe and enough openness for them to express themselves. The staff involved also strove to create an atmosphere of mystery and excitement that held the kids' interest.

After meeting regularly for a couple of months, we decided to hold a ceremony to formally initiate the residents into the order as full-fledged members. They were told in advance, though, that they had to have the Pillars of Character and the meaning of the fist and the hand memorized and be prepared to answer questions about these if they wished to be members. They were clearly very nervous. Many important men in their lives, including teachers, case managers,

Figure 8–1

THE CODE OF THE FIST AND THE HAND:
SELF-CONTROL AND BROTHERHOOD

therapists, and employers were invited. The room was lit by candles, and each initiate had to come up in front of all the men assembled to recite the Pillars of Character and answer questions about the meaning of being a member of the Order of the Fist and the Hand. As each initiate succeeded, he was given a certificate, a symbolic necklace, and a T-shirt with the Order's logo on it. Following this, the assembled

Figure 8-2

THE SIX PILLARS OF CHARACTER

Trustworthiness

Respect for others

Responsibility

Fairness

Caring

Citizenship

"elders" pounded on a table with their fists and then held out their hands as a sign of brotherhood.

The young men's pride at having successfully entered this order based on character was very moving. I reflected on how each of them had internalized so many violent images and destructive values as a young child. I felt heartened that here, at least in these moments, something life-affirming and good was also making its way in.

9

THE ORDER OF THE FIST AND THE HAND—PART II:

Social Issues, Ritual, and Imagery in Group Process

As suggested in the previous chapter, our individual sense of self and self-worth is shaped to a great extent by socially conditioned images that are introjected at an early age. We are often unaware of the visual images that shade our value system and self-concept. Yet if we consider who we wanted to be like as a child, or who we presently admire, we come in contact with the standards and values against which we measure ourselves, which often determine how we speak, dress, work, play, eat, worship, and ultimately how we feel about ourselves. Regardless of how we come by our internal imagery or how conscious we are of it, there can be no doubt about its impact on our lives. This is just as true for individuals with disabilities, and is particularly relevant to adolescents who are groping their way through the developmental stage of identity versus identity diffusion (Erikson 1939). The adolescent's sense of self is very fragile indeed, and highly susceptible to the forces of peer pressure and the pervasive imagery of the media. This was one of our primary considerations when we began formal meetings of the group called the Order of the Fist and the Hand. It was an attempt to see if negative social learning could be counterbalanced by positive milieu effects based on mythical imagery that we hoped would inspire, transform, or at least provide an alternative to gang culture and other expressions of antisocial modeling. We found that the imagery we had invoked through the educational approach had been successful in conveying the ideals and values of self-control and brotherhood, but that a formal group that met once a week would help these young men process internal conflicts and differences among themselves.

Dually diagnosed teenagers with a history of abuse and economic deprivation can present a formidable challenge to group leaders. There will be a tendency for participants to consciously or unconsciously recreate the environment from which they came—hence the structure of the group is critical to keep it from becoming too chaotic. If the group is to be a place that is safe and fosters trust among members, the following issues should be resolved at the outset: confidentiality, lateness, toileting needs, smoking, refreshment needs, name calling, put downs, leaving group because of strong feelings, sleeping, shouting, physical violence, absence, the use of "calm times," absence of group leaders, the process of admitting new members, and the process of leaving the group. A consensus, begrudging or otherwise, must be arrived at so that participants feel they have helped create a structure that is theirs. In the process of doing this, there will be indications of the degree to which various members are positively motivated and are able to "take ownership" of consensual agreements and established norms.

Atmosphere and *ritual* had powerful effects on the behavior and interactions of the members of the Order of the Fist and the Hand. The teasing, bickering, and grandiose posturing that typified the behavior of these youngsters was left at the door of the group room. Members were greeted at the door by one of the group leaders, who reminded them to be still and silent. They entered the room one by one, and were seated at a circular table by the assistant group leader, who did not speak, communicating only by gestures and nods. The room was dark, with blinds drawn, and on the table were six candles representing the Six Pillars of Character. The tablecloth had a print of medieval themes with knights, castles, and dragons. In the center of the table lay a silver scepter with an ornately engraved handle. Sandalwood incense and soft medieval music added to the ambiance, which was enhanced by the rule of silence prior to the opening ritual. Posted on a wall in large Gothic script were the Code of the Order (which was comprised of the Six Pillars of Character listed in Chapter 8) and Rules of Conduct, which were as follows:

RULES OF CONDUCT

1. Speak only when holding the scepter.
2. Ask permission to leave the table.
3. Always make a positive statement before a negative statement.
4. Always respect your brothers in speech and action.

The meeting began in silence. Participants placed the palms of both hands flat on the table and took three slow, deep belly breaths (there had previously been formal instruction in diaphragmatic breathing). Then the group rose together, each member raising his right hand in a fist and his left hand with the palm open, while the leader intoned: "Welcome to the Order of the Fist and the Hand."

Leader: What is the fist?
Group: Self-control.
Leader: What is the hand?
Group: Brotherhood.
Leader: Well done.

Everyone then took their seats, again laid their hands on the table, took three more breaths, made eye contact with all present, and prepared to set the agenda.

One of the main purposes of the ritual was to create intensity and an atmosphere of curiosity and respect. To engage these young men, we felt that it was important that they perceive the Order as special and interesting, and that membership in some way enhanced their social status. Thus it was also important that they feel it was a privilege to belong. Back in the 'hood there was no shortage of charismatic gang leaders waiting to provide an opportunity to belong, feel special, and carry a gun to experience the excitement of carrying the power of life and death in their hands.

The Order fulfilled the need to belong for nearly all the participants. The imagery of knighthood, jousting, the search for the Holy Grail, and battles of good against evil captivated their imagination. They found it exciting to go somewhere special every week where they spoke in secrecy and wore a unique necklace that set them apart from their peers. Coming from chaotic family backgrounds, the ritualistic orderliness and clear limit setting was for many a unique and refreshing experience. However, the "gangsta" imagery and lifestyle of the 'hood was never far away. It was on MTV and the latest CDs, and could be sustained even in their present circumstances through the way they spoke and dressed. Old values and habits die hard, and this struggle of competing images was a recurrent theme of the group. In one meeting it reached a high point due to a school ban on "gangsta" apparel. Danny, a vocal 15-year-old from Watts, had the following comment: "No goddamn principal is going to tell me how to wear my hat and wear my pants. He can pull his own pants over his fat ass up to his chest if he wants, but don't be telling me how to wear my pants. He can go to hell!"

"It sounds to me like you're angry because you feel a part of your identity has been taken away," I ventured.

"Stuff is always getting taken away from us," said Juan, angrily grabbing the scepter. He was 15, and had been a ward of the court since the age of five. "We all got treated badly growing up, and we're sick of it. We didn't have no homes, nobody to care about us, and the people we got put with—hell, they treated us worse. People got no idea how that was. We got a right to be angry!"

"I didn't have those experiences," I responded, "but I can empathize with how painful that must have been."

"I don't want you to *emphasize* anything!" he retorted.

"No, empathize—understand how it was for you."

"Well, I can tell you one thing—you can't fix all that's gone wrong with big words. We're just tired of feeling ripped off all the time."

I noticed that Michael, an African-American youth who had come a long way in learning how to cope with his anger (see Chapter 2) was motioning for the scepter so that he could speak. "You guys got a major attitude problem," he began. "I don't like no fool of a principal telling me what I can wear and not wear, but I ain't ready to start a war over it. You gotta use some self-control. That's what we mean by the fist—self-control, man. You use some self-control and you don't blow it. You wanna get kicked out and go back to Juvenile Hall or be back out in the street, be my guest, man. You soon be one more dead brother like I saw on TV in the news last night."

Self-control was no abstract matter for Michael. His explosive temper had caused him to be removed last year from his grandmother's home where he had lived for several months with his two sisters. He loved his grandmother very much and was hoping to have another chance at family reunification. His success with his anger management program was supporting that hope. It was not always easy for him, but it was apparent that the imagery, ritual, and support of the Order gave him an opportunity to feel good about himself by assuming a leadership role with others. I noticed, however, that Danny had been staring angrily at me as Michael was speaking.

"It looks like you've got something on your mind, Danny," I said. "What's up?"

Danny took the scepter, and brandished it for emphasis as he spoke. "What's on my mind is that you white people got no idea about what it's like out there. I spent my whole life watchin' people get messed with. I had to call the cops one time when my dad was beating my mother half to death. Then the cops came and took him away. Then comes a social worker and takes me away. You white people are always telling other people how to run their life, but you got no idea what their life is like."

Michael had been making a large effort not to interrupt as Danny was speaking, but managed to contain himself and asked Danny if he could speak to him in a "personal" way. Danny groaned, and nodded reluctantly.

"I can see that you're hurtin', brother," he said. "We all hurtin' here. That's why we talk about brotherhood—to help each other. Stayin' mad at white people won't make you feel better. That's what we come here for every week—to learn how to get along better with each other—and that includes white people. They always be here, brother, and we got to find ways to live with them."

The ideal of brotherhood was always in counterpoint to the spontaneous expression of racial tension that erupted in the group, as it so frequently does in society at large. Putting down people of different color or ethnic origin was a reflexive interactional pattern that we tried to make more conscious in the group, so that members could become aware that their quickness to put down others was a way of not getting hurt first, and ultimately an attempt to compensate for low self-esteem. Nevertheless, the racial tensions in the real world outside were often a matter of life and death, and we could not underestimate the significance of this. I told Danny that he was right about the street life being different from how we related in the Order, but that he had the power to choose a way of relating to others that made him feel good about himself and allowed others to feel good about themselves. Danny impatiently stated that he knew what I was talking about, and that he had had a bad day at school. I then changed the pace by asking if anyone would like to share a secret hope they had about something they wanted to do but weren't able to do. Larry, a quiet Chinese-American, surprised me by talking about his desire to locate his father, whom he believed to be a powerful leader of a Chinese triad in San Francisco. He had not seen or heard from his father for over ten years, but he was convinced he could find him if he could only get to Chinatown. When I asked him what he would do to support himself in San Francisco he stated blandly that he would join a Chinese gang, and if he had to kill someone to get in, that was no problem for him. When I said that he would probably end up in jail, his reply was, "Then maybe I'll meet my father, 'cause that's where he probably is. My social worker always says he's either in jail somewhere or dead. But I know he's not dead. He's too smart to be dead. He's the leader of a triad, and they take care of each other."

Larry then passed the scepter to David, a 16-year-old red-headed youth with an intense and deliberate manner of speaking. He began by telling Larry he had an important message for him if he was ready to hear it. Larry folded his arms defiantly and nodded. Oblivious of the double message that had just been conveyed, David said, "Larry, first I'm going to follow the rule of saying the positive first. You know, you're a nice quiet Chinese guy. You mind your own business and you never bug anybody. But you shocked the shit out of me just now. You been sitting here in this group for three months now, agreeing with the Code and being a member of the Order, so how can you just start talking about jail, killing, and all? I can see you wanting to find your dad, but it sounds to me like he's long gone. I wish I had a dad too, but I ain't got one. I got some screwed up relatives who are in and out of jail, but just because they're my relatives it doesn't mean that they can help me. We're all lookin' for something, but we gotta find something that makes our life better, not worse. Don't do anything that hurts people, man, because you'll never feel good inside if you do. You gotta stop and think about what makes you feel good inside, and I think that living by the Code makes you feel good inside. You got some bad pictures in your head, man, and you got to get rid of them. That's what I need to say to you, and thanks for listening."

The exchange between Larry and David gave some indication of what their respective inner dialogues must be like. I saw over a period of several months that, for Larry, the images and ideals of the group were not strong enough to help him break out of the orbit of past longings and the self-talk that fueled them. Like Danny, it was hard for him to disidentify from the violent images that had shaped him and had become associated with the lure of the street. The battle of competing images, fantasies, and longings went on within the hearts of each member of the group and was obvious at times. Of the eight members of this particular group, about half remained relatively untouched by the imagery and ideals of the Order over a six-month period. The other half were able to make self-control and brotherhood relevant in their lives. They came to the group with the motivation and desire to change and used the opportunity to do so.

What happened in this group was very much like what happens in every arena of life. Some benefit from situations in which there is honesty, trust, and the sharing of positive ideals, and others do not. As society at large has not provided the leadership and resources to cope with most of the social ills illustrated above, one cannot expect miracles from an experimental therapy group. However, I am happy to say that the Order of the Fist and the Hand continued and many new members came to envision life in a more positive way as they developed within themselves a more wholesome self-image and tried as best they could to express the ideals of self-control and brotherhood in their daily life.

10

DRAMATIC OVERTURES:

Working with the Histrionic Personality

Tina had black, short-cropped hair, intense brown eyes, and greeted everyone like long-lost relatives. There were very few words she could enunciate completely, and her sentences were a patchwork of half-formed syllables, swallowed words, and catchy phrases, which she combined with wild gestures and flailing leg movements. During our first meeting I responded positively to what I could understand of her speech. However, Tina reacted to almost everything I said with woeful sounds, hand wringing, or an explosion of tears. At one point during the session, she simply slid off her chair and collapsed on the floor. By the middle of the session, I did manage to figure out that she liked to go to McDonald's and wanted her medication changed. Then, during the first quiet moment of comfortable understanding, Tina exposed her breasts, shouting "Look! Look!" When I made it very clear that this was not acceptable, Tina attempted to induce vomiting, and kicked my kneecap. I was very grateful when the session was over, and I had a surge of empathy for Tina's parents and teachers.

Tina was referred to me for individual psychotherapy because her churchgoing Roman Catholic parents were at a loss as to how to manage her most recent behavior, which was to pull up her skirt in public, and shout "Look at me!" Teachers and aides at Tina's school were also highly alarmed. However, what became apparent to me after my first few sessions with Tina was that the greater the intensity of reaction she elicited, the more her behavior was reinforced. Punishments involving the loss of privileges, special snacks, or fun activities didn't bother Tina a bit; negative consequences were, for Tina, tangible proof that her behavior had created the desired effect. There was a certain glee that came into Tina's eyes when she was being provocative, as if she were just waiting for you to lose it.

I experimented with not reacting to Tina's exhibitionistic behaviors by simply turning my head away and being silent. For the most part this was quite effective. At times she would look pained and say, "You not like me? Mad?" When I assured her that I did like her she would break out in a broad smile and say: "I love you. You my boyfriend. Marry me." Initially it was difficult to keep Tina at arm's length, and at times I felt that working with her was a lawsuit in the making. However, it soon became clear to me that Tina's exhibitionism was not at all sexual. It was **histrionic** with the goal of getting attention. Tina was attempting to elicit an energetic intensity that matched her own, and how she did that depended on who she was relating to.

Behavioral interventions were certainly needed in this case, but a careful review of Tina's file indicated that Tina had outmaneuvered one token economy and reinforcement schedule after another, and had demonstrated relative immunity to all contingency systems of short- and long-term rewards and consequences. Tina had been given the diagnosis of Pervasive Developmental Disorder NOS and Mild Mental Retardation, but it seemed to me that there was a diagnostic piece missing. The *DSM-IV* diagnostic guidelines do not allow the assignment of personality disorders to anyone under the age of 18, but it was my observation that Tina, at the age of 16, was exhibiting many behaviors related to Histrionic Personality Disorder. Millon (1996), a prolific writer in the field of personality disorders, and a member of the *DSM-IV* Axis II Work Group, describes this personality as follows:

> Although not unique, there are distinctive aspects to the expressive behaviors of histrionics. They are overreactors, relating at times in a

volatile and a provocative manner, but usually displaying themselves in an engaging and theatrical manner. They show a tendency to be intolerant of inactivity, resulting in impulsive, capricious, and highly emotional behaviors. . . . histrionic personalities tend to be easily excited, and intolerant of frustration, delay, and disappointment. Moreover, the words and feelings they express appear shallow and simulated rather than deep or real. [p. 367]

In taking a **psychodynamic** perspective my intention was to understand Tina more completely by taking into account aspects of personality and interpersonal style underlying her behavior. Tina was a multifaceted individual with a vitality and sparkle that was unique. However there was what Millon calls a "tempestuous" and "exaggerated" quality to her expression of feeling, which seemed to be related to her need to be the center of attention wherever she went. There was a desperation to Tina's theatrics, which I surmised was due in large part to her disability. Tina did not have a way to process or understand the rapidly shifting feelings that erupted within her and, unlike higher functioning histrionics, she was unable to enchant or seduce those from whom she wanted attention and affection. I believed that Tina's bizarre and unpredictable behaviors were desperate attempts to communicate the intensity of her inner pain, which for most histrionics is related to the fear of abandonment and the inability to tolerate aloneness.

Tina frequently conveyed to me that my main job was to get her psychiatrist to change her medication and that the three of us should meet at lunchtime every week. In an elliptical manner, she also led me to understand that I could be of service by arranging meetings with me, her family, psychiatrist, and teacher so that we could all talk about how to help her. She intimated that counseling time might best be used to go to McDonald's for large fries and a coke.

By setting and vigorously maintaining clear boundaries with Tina, her dramatic behavior became manageable. Our work was enhanced by a positive **transference** which was managed by setting very explicit behavioral limits in session with a good deal of room for spontaneous playfulness. Tina could not put coherent sentences together to express her thoughts and feelings, but she always found a way to make her point. I often sustained rapport with her by way of singing familiar songs and doing simple breathing exercises. As Tina's behavior usually caused those in her environment to reject her, a good deal of her acting out was a test to see how much someone could tolerate. Underlying this was a longing to be accepted and understood. But given the impact Tina's current behavior had on others, her need for acceptance could not be fulfilled without considerable behavioral change. To facilitate this change I formulated therapeutic objectives as illustrated in Figure 10–1, which I shared with Tina's teacher and family.

Figure 10–1

TINA'S THERAPEUTIC GOALS AND ACTIVITIES

(For Teachers and Parents Working with Histrionic Personality Styles)

1. Teach Tina to sustain her focus of attention on one thing and thought at a time.
2. Interrupt Tina when she self-distracts and abruptly shifts attention when speaking and playing. Ask her to explain what has just become more interesting to her.
3. Model clear and complete thinking by having Tina choose a topic of interest and have a brief but complete reciprocal exchange.
4. Increase association between thoughts, feelings, and behavior with drawings, words, and pictures that fit together.
5. Help Tina to modulate labile affect. Teach her how to slow down by way of relaxation exercises. Have her count the number of feelings she has in a given interval.
6. Model solid, respectful, boundaried relationships.
7. Help Tina discriminate between authentic feelings and the inauthentic dramatizations she employs to shock people and coerce them into giving her what she wants.

When working with the developmentally disabled, it is important to share key insights and effective interventions with families, educators, and other professionals involved in care. The issue of confidentiality is delicate, but it can be managed judiciously and respectfully by discussing the matter openly with clients and families. Children and adolescents with disabilities need help across settings with great consistency, and no amount of individual and group therapy can be a substitute for this. To help Tina's teachers and parents with therapeutic goal Number 7, I created a Communication Board with the pictures illustrated in Figure 10–2.

One of the purposes of the communication board was to help translate Tina's *I want* statements into *I feel* statements. For example, it was common for Tina to ask a family member to take her to McDonald's after she had finished a substantial meal. Tina would hold her belly, moan that she was hungry, frown, say she was starving, cry, drool, hold her face in her hands, sigh, wring her hands, and interrupt whoever she was talking to with unceasing demands to go to McDonald's. It was natural for the family to feel helpless and become reactive. But with the Communication Board there was something that they could physically use. It was also a bridge from the therapy office to the parents, who had feelings of shame, guilt, and inadequacy that were weighing heavily on them. With something concrete to work with, they felt more hopeful and became more receptive to understanding Tina's behavior. Tina liked the board because it was another way of getting attention. Underlying Tina's histrionic way of relating was a strong desire to engage with others, a vitality and spontaneity that were positive personal qualities.

Tina's family, to their credit, had always been appreciative of her underlying strengths. In one meeting they explained her medication history. Six months prior to my involvement, Tina's teachers felt it was impossible to work with her, and the school had planned to expel her. To make her behavior more manageable she was given a high dosage of tranquilizing medication. During that period, according to her parents, her eyes lost their luster and she walked around in something like a "zombie-like daze," well behaved but without a trace of her former vitality. Her parents were so shocked by this that they had the

Figure 10–2

BOARD FOR GENUINE COMMUNICATION

(When Tina gets 'stuck' on a particular topic, when you think that there may be a deeper feeling beneath what she's saying or doing, and/or when you are having a significant personal reaction to her actions toward you, use the following communication board as a tool to deepen your interpersonal interaction with her.)

Tina -- *I Feel*:

Staff -- *I Feel*:

Figure 10–2 (continued)

sad

I want excitement

hungry

happy

homesick

Yeah!

medication discontinued and let the psychiatrist do a trial of Ritalin, which also proved ineffective. What I inferred from this was that Tina discriminated differences in her internal state when she was on various medication trials, and learned at a bodily level that medication could in fact change the way she felt. This explained to me why she was so eager for me to arrange meetings with her psychiatrist; I believed that in her "drugged-out" state she had experienced relief from her intensely conflicted inner state, and came to feel that something or someone outside of herself could provide a solution to her problems. However, her parents preferred a wild and unruly Tina to a sleepwalking Tina. A nondemonstrative family with a controlled communication style, they loved Tina very much and tolerated her excesses. As I got to know them better it became clear that their expression of love for Tina was a matter of still waters running very deep. It also appeared that Tina was the "spark plug," the expressive force in this family system.

The therapeutic task of helping Tina discriminate between authentic feelings and the dramatized feelings she used to coerce attention from those around her was a difficult one. However, modest gains were made by the use of playful **empathic reflection** in conjunction with the communication board. What follows are segments of dialogue from a typical session.

> *Tina:* I want . . . see Doctor . . . you come with me . . . med change. . . .
> *Dr. Campbell:* I'll call him for you.
> *Tina:* [frowning, slapping her leg impatiently] No, no! *Meet* him. You . . . me . . . go together . . . [smiling] med change.
> *Dr. Campbell:* [mirroring smile] You're a great social arranger, Tina. Every week you want me to meet someone else. You like to have lots of people meeting and talking about you. Show me on your communication board what you're feeling now.
> *Tina:* [irritated] No board! . . . McDonald's! McDonalds! Hungry!
> *Dr. Campbell:* Show me on the board what you're feeling now.
> *Tina:* Sad!

Dr. Campbell: Show me the sad picture.

Tina: [points, acting sad] Sad!

Dr. Campbell: I think you get a lot of attention when you act sad, then you forget what you really feel. Oh goodness, what can we do about that?

Tina: [pouting] Hungry!

Dr. Campbell: Point to a picture.

Tina: [points to angry picture] Happy!

Dr. Campbell: Really? Now I'm all confused. I wonder if you're also confused about how you feel? Why don't you show me how Pocahontas looks when she's happy.

Tina: No! Cinderella!

Dr. Campbell: Well, hello, Cinderella—I love your beautiful white gown.

Tina: [jumping up and parading around] Cinderella, Cinderella, Cinderella. . . .

Dr. Campbell: [clapping] All right! Now turn Cinderella into Tina.

Tina: Now Cinderella [waving an imaginary wand] . . . now Tina.

Dr. Campbell: [clapping] Great! But now it's midnight and the ball is over! Sit down and put the picture board on your lap. That's right! Give me the picture that shows how you feel.

Tina: [out of breath from dancing around, offers the happy face picture]

The preceding sequence reflected the importance of staying with attentional shifts and following Tina's energy and interests to do whatever was necessary to keep Tina engaged. Although words and pictures were used to communicate, there was a good deal of nonverbal exchange during which Tina felt she was understood and accepted, even though she did not always get the response she wanted to her emotional displays and demands.

As Tina developed a greater capacity to attend and concentrate, and as the adults in her life learned to ignore her exhibitionism, her acting out behaviors diminished in frequency and duration. Tina was eventually able to do structured role play. Later, Tina was accepted in a drama group for adolescents with disabilities, a structured and creative venue in which she received ample recognition and attention for the expressive side of her personality.

For many children, behavioral acting out is the only way they know to gain attention or assert their autonomy and identity, so these behaviors continue, regardless of negative consequences. We can't take these behaviors away without replacing them with something else. And we can't really provide lasting help until we go beyond the notion of changing and shaping behavior and fully commit ourselves to understanding the person behind the behavior and the ways her behavior functions for her. Tina's behaviors, which were typical of the histrionic personality style, were the extreme measures she felt she had to take to obtain attention, acknowledgment, and material gain from her immediate environment. The histrionic aspect of her personality can be simply understood as a way that Tina once learned to cope and get her needs met. Her disability made the dysfunctional aspect more extreme.

Tina's need for attention did not decrease significantly during my work with her but, due to her sparkling charm and basic good humor, she learned new ways to get most of the attention she needed without shocking people and making such a fuss. Her struggle to discriminate between authentic and inauthentic feelings continued. Often a stern word or glance elicited a coy smile, and it was clear that she knew she had been "caught." She would then good-naturedly move on to the next dramatic overture and measure its effect.

11

AGGRESSION AND PROJECTIVE IDENTIFICATION:

Working with Splitting and Projective Identification

One afternoon, I was meeting with Jim Woodard at his office in the Omega House to discuss Paola, an energetic, 12-year-old resident whom I was seeing for individual psychotherapy. Just as Jim was telling me about how severe Paola's aggressive and tantrum behaviors had become over recent weeks, we heard her screaming.

As we walked toward the living room, I could hear a staff member named Susan, who was working with Paola, use as soothing a voice as she could. "It's okay, Paola. Come sit down with me. Come on and we can talk."

Paola shouted, "Why you doing stuff to me, always bugging me? I can't stand it!" Then she screamed at the top of her lungs, grabbing Susan's hand and pinching into the skin. Susan quickly pulled her hand back and moved away from Paola. Paola followed her, shouting, "Why can't you leave me alone?"

As they moved into the dining room, Paola continued screaming and began knocking over one chair after another. She kicked a chair and then lunged at Susan who moved behind a table.

I then stepped into Paola's peripheral vision and, with the intent of distracting her from attacking again, I said, "Paola, hello." She turned towards me and, panting from her exertion, said, "Hi. I'm upset."

She then turned back toward Susan, whom she'd been chasing, and began screaming again. I moved a step closer to her and, gesturing away from the staff, said, "Paola, would you like to come this way?"

She moved toward me until she was just one step away. Then, looking directly into my eyes, she let out a gut-wrenching scream that nearly knocked me over. I recall feeling less fear than awe at the sheer energy and strength that this thin little girl could muster.

When the scream finally ended, Paola was still looking me in the eyes. She tried to say something but had begun hyperventilating. She leaned over, resting her arm on one of the chairs she'd tipped over. Her body was shaking. I put my hand on her shoulder and said, "I hear you. Come and sit down."

During our individual sessions, Paola had been surprisingly pleasant, often charming. She would draw very sweet pictures of colorful animals, flowers, or happy family scenes. She seemed to enjoy playing with sandtray toys or talking about daily events, dreams, or hopes for her future, though these interactions did sometimes seem hollow or superficial. When I asked her about aggressive episodes like the one described above, she would sometimes become unwilling to talk, though at other times she would express regret, briefly discuss other ways she could have behaved, and then attempt to change the subject.

Paola was born in Arizona, and her father abandoned her mother when she was 2. She had a close, somewhat protective relationship with her mother, who had been overwhelmed by trying to raise a developmentally disabled child along with two other daughters and a son. Paola was diagnosed as having Mild Mental Retardation and **Attention-deficit Hyperactivity Disorder (ADHD).** There were reports that either an uncle or the maternal grandfather had molested Paola and one of her sisters. It also seemed that she had often been left with her siblings, who had sometimes abandoned her or locked her in a small bedroom when she'd acted out. She had been placed at Omega House by the county mental health agency in response to her mother's request for assistance. Her mother did come to visit Paola, though not as frequently as either of them would have liked.

Jim Woodard had asked me to visit with him on the afternoon mentioned above because he and his staff were concerned and confused about how to effectively help Paola. They had tried talking directly with Paola about her behavioral incidents and had implemented a number of behavioral contracts, but episodes much longer and more severe than the one described above were still occurring at a rate of one to three times per day.

At their next staff meeting, I asked Susan about the **antecedents** to the incident I had witnessed. She explained that they had been making a salad for dinner when she'd noticed that Paola was somewhat agitated. She admitted that she'd become somewhat anxious on noticing this, as she was very familiar with how aggressive Paola could become when agitated. She had tried to distract her by talking about an upcoming trip to an amusement park, hoping to cheer her up. However, Paola's agitation had continued escalating, as indicated by her sighing, hitting the counter a couple of times, and giving the staff dirty looks. When Susan dropped a fork, Paola began screaming about how the staff always "bugged her," "yelled at her," and were "mean" to her. Susan then backed into the living room to get Paola away from the sharp objects in the kitchen—and that was the point at which we had come in.

I learned that incidents of this kind were common. For example, when Paola was playing together with other girls, she would easily become agitated. Then, if another girl brushed lightly against her arm or laughed spontaneously, Paola would often begin shouting that the girl was "hitting me," "cursing at me," or "being mean to me." These shouts would quickly be followed by hair pulling, scratching, and hitting. Both the supervisor and the staff with whom I spoke were obviously upset by these behaviors and very much wanted to help Paola to get better.

Given my own experience in therapy with Paola, my knowledge of her history, and my observations of her interactions with her staff, I realized our work with her would benefit from an understanding of the psychological mechanisms of **projective identification** and **splitting**. Because many children with developmental disabilities and/or abusive backgrounds use projective identification and splitting in order to deal with overwhelming feelings and to relate or communicate with others, I have become increasingly convinced that a basic practical understanding of these mechanisms can be extremely useful for parents, therapists, teachers, and other caregivers.

Both splitting and projective identification are normal psychological processes, essential to a child's development of a healthy ego and healthy interpersonal relations. However, when neurological problems are present and/or there is a history of abuse and neglect, a child may rely too heavily on these mechanisms as a defense, thereby inhibiting psychosocial development.

Put simply, splitting is a process whereby a person separates good from bad, nurturing from threatening, love from hate. This happens because the bad, frightening, or hateful appears so overwhelming that it threatens to destroy the hold a child has on what is pleasurable, nurturing, and positive. A child who relies on splitting is very much in the moment; things are "all good" and happy or become "all bad," leading to feelings of rage or overwhelming fear.

One could see this mechanism functioning quite clearly in Paola's relationships. Paola enjoyed her therapy sessions and saw me as a positive, nurturing figure. The characters in the drawings and the stories she made up during play were always happy, the scenes idyllic. When I would bring up some negative incident or feeling, she would either become silent or give whatever answer she guessed I wanted to hear in order to quickly change the subject. It was as if she did not want to contaminate our good relationship with these bad feelings or images. Even during her rageful episode in the dorm, when she saw me, she paused to say, "Hi. I'm upset." She did not attack or blame me as she did her staff. Two typical aspects of splitting that we see in Paola are her *idealizing* some people and relationships while *devaluing* others, and her "selective lack of impulse control" (Gabbard 1994, p. 45).

When a child who is unconsciously using splitting as a defense mechanism is in a family, classroom, and/or group home setting, if adult caregivers are not aware of this, then it is all too common for disagreements, inconsistencies, and confusion to ensue. One can imagine how easy and tempting it would be for someone in the "good" role, as I was, to wind up *blaming* the staff for Paola's aggressive and tantrum behaviors. (In fact, blaming other professionals or caregivers for a child's problems is often a "red flag" to check whether we may have gotten caught up in a countertransference reaction to a child's splitting process.) Conversely, those toward whom the child acts out can easily come to feel that others don't really understand the child or are incompetent. I have seen many cases where such splits between different caregivers in a child's life were not dealt with well, leading to negative long-term effects for the child. In Paola's case, it was good that the supervisor of the group home had asked me to come to talk with him and his staff. Through a number of discussions at their staff meetings, we were able to discover that, even within the group home staff team, there were disagreements about what Paola needed and how staff should work with her. Had her adult caregivers not resolved these issues consciously, through dialogue, then they might have unwittingly acted out Paola's internal world of split dichotomies, thereby reinforcing her ultimately unhealthy way of seeing and interacting with the external world.

This tendency of therapists, teachers, or caregivers to inadvertently act out a child's inner conflicts is often encouraged by the child's use of **projective identification**, a psychological mechanism that often accompanies splitting. A useful way of introducing the concept of projective identification is by comparing it with the more familiar phenomenon of projection (see Figure 11-1). In *projection*, one attributes an aspect of one's own internal world to another person. For example, I once worked with a paranoid man who sat in his room for hours perseverating on how his neighbors were plotting to kill him. This man had projected his own internal aggressive or self-destructive fantasies onto his neighbors. A teenage crush is another familiar example of projection; idealized romantic fantasies are projected onto a selected peer or adult, which is followed by reverie and daydreaming but rarely by contact. In contrast, one might say that *projective identification* is more active and relational. In *projective identification*, one unconsciously imagines that an aspect of one's inner world has been projected *into* and exists inside of someone else,

Figure 11–1

PROJECTION

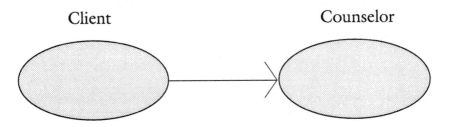

Client   Counselor

Attributes unwanted aspects of self *onto* counselor.

PROJECTIVE IDENTIFICATION

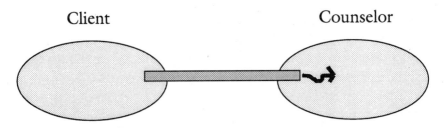

Client   Counselor

In fantasy, client projects unmanageable aspects of self *into* counselor and tries to control these by controlling counselor.

and one then tries to *control* this aspect of oneself by trying to control the other person.

Both positive and negative aspects of the self can be dealt with through projective identification. As an example of positive projective identification, in her relationship with me, Paola had projected her inner image of a nurturing and loving presence onto me. She then acted in a very sweet way with me in order to evoke positive, caring feelings. Paola's positive image of a loving, caring presence came from those times when her mother had not felt overwhelmed and was able to spend quality time with her. However, in reality, siblings, financial difficulties, abusive relatives, and Paola's own attentional difficulties and aggressive tendencies had too often marred these positive moments, and so Paola projected some of these positive feelings and images onto me, hoping that I might keep them safe. In fact, she often asked me to hold onto drawings she had done of happy family scenes, and she would later ask to see that I had kept them safe and intact.

In negative projective identification, an overwhelming all-bad aspect of the child's self arises and the child finds this intolerable. (See Figure 11–2 for an overview of how negative projective identification works.) In Paola's case, a number of the staff with whom I spoke said that they could see her becoming agitated prior to aggressive episodes. Given her history, it would not be surprising that she would have unbearable internal images regarding neglect and abuse along with feelings of rage. Because Paola couldn't bear these feelings, she would project them onto a caregiver or peer in her immediate environment. Her aggressive episodes generally began with shouting about how someone else had hit her, had been "bugging" her, or had been mean to her. Although her peers or caregivers might actually have been quite calm and happy—playing or making a salad for dinner—Paola was subjectively perceiving them as being cruel, invasive, or aggressive. By then acting in a blaming and aggressive way, Paola often evoked genuinely invasive and aggressive reactions from her peers. Ironically, this would often calm her down somewhat, as she would then go tell on the peer, in a sense proving that her projection was correct. In her interactions with staff, her aggressions would often escalate to a level requiring them to physically restrain her in order to

Figure 11–2

SUMMARY OF
NEGATIVE PROJECTIVE IDENTIFICATION:

How it works:
1) Highly anxiety-producing, potentially overwhelming aspect of the client's inner world arises.
2) Client finds this experience unbearable.
3) Client projects this unbearable aspect of himself onto someone else.
4) Client then acts so as to evoke the feelings or behaviors associated with this aspect of himself in the other person.

He is using others to try to cope with and manage his overwhelming internal states. He is also often re-creating former chaotic interpersonal relations that he introjected during childhood.

Given this, Projective Identification may serve as:
1) A way the client communicates about aspects of himself.
2) A way of relating with others. We all relate in this way at times. Doing so frequently is a function of unclear but developing interpersonal (self/other) boundaries.
3) An opportunity for change, if the other person (e.g., the therapist) can process what the client has projected and reintroduce it to the client in a way that he can understand and manage.

Counselor's options:
1) Block the client from communicating in this way (e.g., by remaining dedicated or loving without having to understand the complexity and negativity of the client). This tends to lead to further escalation in order for other to "get it."
2) Feel what the patient evokes in you and then act out those feelings.
3) Recognize how and why the client may be relating with you in this way. Recognize what the patient may be communicating and why. Process (digest) evoked feelings internally and then decide how to use your understanding of the client therapeutically with the client (e.g., through interpretation, empathic reflection, etc.).

keep her from hurting them. Again, once she had forced them to use force, she would often begin calming down.

During a staff meeting that I attended, a large percentage of the staff reported negative feelings about having to get involved in these incidents. They found it particularly difficult when, during physical restraints, Paola would often continue her accusations: "You're mean to me! Why you doing this stuff to me? You're abusing me!" A few sensitive staff said that although they knew that they were doing the best that they could for her, after the restraints they sometimes felt as if they had been abusive. In reviewing both Figure 11–1 and Figure 11–2 with the staff, we discussed how their own feelings were related to Paola's use of projective identification. We talked about the importance of not blaming her and of recognizing how she was inadvertently re-creating many of the unpleasant interactional patterns that had traumatized her in the past. We also talked about how the staff's experiences of these unpleasant feelings could be a useful way of developing a deeper level of empathy for Paola.

A collaborative and empathic approach is essential when working with children who use splitting and projective identification. However, deciding on how to actually intervene with them is not easy. Wilfred Bion (1977) discusses how projective identification and associated behavioral acting out serve as substitutes for learning and thinking. Because the child feels overwhelmed by affects and experiences, he splits and acts out; this prevents him from having the time and space necessary for thinking about his experiences and learning from them. A practical way of working with someone who uses projective identification is helping him to turn overwhelming experiences and sensations into thoughts, words, and memories. Being able to think about our feelings and experiences is essential in not becoming overwhelmed by them and having to act out.

In my work with Paola, I helped her to identify bodily feelings and mental images that arose when she became agitated. Her staff also began discussing these issues with her. We developed a covert reinforcement sequence to teach her alternative ways of reacting when she recognized these thoughts or feelings (see Figure 11–3). Her staff reviewed this sequence with her daily and reminded her of these options as soon as they noticed any agitation on her part. Note that of the three reactive choices that were being encouraged, only one (playing soccer in the yard) was truly a distraction from the source of agitation. We felt that it was important to give her an option of doing a favorite physical activity to release energy and distract herself if she wanted to. The other two options—playing with special toys or talking with staff—were designed to give her ways of processing (through words or play images) the kinds of overwhelming thoughts and feelings that would otherwise lead to her acting out. Her staff also decided that if she did begin feeling agitated and then used one of these positive options rather than acting out, they would reinforce her with praise and by taking her on special outings.

We also decided that when Paola was doing well with a given staff member—having a positive, all-good interaction—they could at times share with her some of their reflections and feelings about past negative interactions. Again, they were encouraged to use "I" statements. For example, they might say, "I felt hurt (or sad, angry, etc.) the other day when you shouted at me." The idea here was to try to bridge her split between good and bad, reintroducing tolerable (psychologically digested) bits of "bad" during positive interactions.

One thing that was particularly helpful in my work with her was discussing how some of the problematic patterns in her current relationships were based on earlier ones. Given her cognitive deficits, complex insights in this regard were not possible. However, she was particularly able to understand how her hitting or "being mean" to smaller peers was similar to how her older siblings had treated her.

I believe that it is important to state that none of the interventions described above brought about sudden or dramatic progress. In fact, for clients who use these kinds of defense mechanisms, dramatic progress is often false progress. However, the frequency of Paola's aggressive episodes did gradually decrease over the next few months. Also, as the quality of her relationships with her peers and staff gradually improved, her quality of life improved as well. And when Paola did exhibit emotional irruptions and aggression, her caregivers' deepened empathic understanding of her psychology and behaviors allowed them to more easily tolerate these difficulties.

Figure 11–3

PAOLA'S PERSONAL GROWTH PROGRAM

1. When I'm . . .

(Have her choose one of these three situations and describe as many details as she can.)
1. Playing with my friends—Which friends? What are you doing with them?
2. Coming home from school
3. Doing a task with staff—Which staff? What task?

2. And I begin feeling . . .

(Have her describe how she may feel when agitated. Examples she has mentioned in the past include stomach upset, breathing heavy, "angry for no reason," "want to kick someone," and "like everyone is bugging me.")

3. I can "Stop" and take a deep breath . . .

(Practice saying "Stop" and taking a few deep belly breaths with her.)

4. And I can choose to help myself grow by . . .

1. Talking with favorite staff about how I'm feeling and why.
2. Going to my room to play with my special toys.
3. Going into the yard and playing with the soccer ball.

5. When I do this, I feel good about myself! I imagine myself . . .

(Have her imagine a reenforcing scene, e.g., a beautiful house with trees and lots of animals to play with, like horses, dolphins, hippos, giraffes, etc.)

12

TRUTH OR CONSEQUENCES:

A Values-Based Behavioral Approach

Charlie's father, Ben, contacted me because Charlie was raising the stakes in his battle to ride his bike to school. Charlie's disability, plus the extreme hazard of the route, made this a life-threatening issue. For Charlie it was a matter of self-esteem. All the other kids rode their bikes to school and his pride took a beating each day when he got off the bus and passed the racks of bikes on his way to class. Charlie was 19 years old, lived at home, and attended a special education class during the day. Cerebral palsy had left him with impaired coordination on his left side and an unsteady gait. During our initial phone contact, Ben told me that Charlie's oppositional behavior had escalated with the recent absence of his mother, who had been obliged to remain in Europe with her elderly mother. Ben was a retired Air Force colonel and believed discipline was a key to success in life. He was also a kind and tolerant man, and was doing his best to understand why Charlie was making such a big fuss about riding his bike to school when it had been proven to be an unsafe route for him, given his limited coordination and the busy traffic conditions. Because Charlie had become so argumentative and unruly, Ben had implemented a home-use version of the behavioral target sheet that was used for Charlie at school. "I know that he misses his mother," Ben said emotionally. "He hasn't always been this way, so I know he can pull it together if he wants. If he wants to act up, then he'll be monitored and take the consequences, because that's what happens in real life. Real life is right around the corner for Charlie, and I'm afraid of what will happen when it catches up to him."

Ben agreed to participate in sessions with Charlie, and they both came in a week later. Charlie was a slightly overweight youth, with jet black hair and deeply inset eyes that wandered around the room as he spoke. He had an extremely difficult time sitting still, sustaining eye contact, or responding directly to questions. Ben started to relate the details of their latest argument about the bike riding issue when Charlie suddenly began to intone a medley of Beach Boys songs. Ben looked at me helplessly, so I asked Charlie how his behavior at home had been the past week. He paused for a moment and asked, "Why don't elephants wear shoes?"

After about 20 minutes of scattered discussion punctuated by limericks and songs, I decided to teach Charlie diaphragmatic breathing and perceptual focusing exercises. I suggested that this might make these sessions easier for him and help him with his schoolwork. I was quite moved by his father's volunteering to do the exercises with us so that he would be able to help Charlie practice them at home. This caring participation seemed to touch Charlie as well. His interruptions, disruptions, and slapstick subsided considerably during the last half of the session.

Charlie was then able to tell me that he saw the main problem as being too many rules around the house for a person his age. For example, he felt that someone his age should be able to decide by himself if he wanted to shave in the morning. "And I don't like carrying around this piece of crap at home," he said, showing me his behavioral target sheet (see Figure 12–1).

When I had finished scanning the target sheet I looked up to find Charlie and his father staring intensely at me, as if expecting me to render judgment on the content and use of this hotly contested document.

"It helps keep him in line," Charlie's father said.

"It sucks," said Charlie, glancing apprehensively at his father.

Figure 12-1

CHARLIE'S TARGET SHEET

Evening Targets	3–4 pm	4–5 pm	5–6 pm	6–7 pm	7–8 pm	8–9 pm	9–10 pm

1. Following Directions

2. Polite Speech

3. Respecting Property

* This target sheet is to help Charlie take responsibility for his actions in a mature way, and so that he will follow household rules.

* In order to succeed, Charlie will need to earn a *yes* for 6 of the 8 boxes per shift. If Charlie gets less than 6 *yes* checks he will be grounded for 24 hours.

* If Charlie is grounded while doing the target sheet, the *yes* or *no* for each box will affect his grounding. If Charlie gets a *yes* in a box, his grounding will be reduced by one hour. If Charlie gets a *no* in a box, his grounding will be increased by one hour.

* Charlie will be given one reminder to follow directions. If he follows the directions he earns a *yes* in the box. If he does not follow directions after the second reminder, he will earn a *no* in the box, which will result in being grounded.

* If Charlie is grounded he is not to watch TV or ride his bike, and he must complete 2 hours of chores. For each hour of chores that he completes, he will earn one hour off his grounding.

I told them I would discuss my point of view in more detail at the next session and thanked them both for their willingness to work things out in a friendly way. Of the many directions to take, I felt that the best immediate course was to encourage and support the evolving relationship between father and son and not let theoretical considerations concerning the target sheet get in the way. It was clear that Ben felt that they both needed the target sheet at this time. I lent him a copy of a recent article of Dr. Gary LaVigna's (LaVigna and Willis 1997) on the advantages of positive programming over punishment. Dr. La Vigna wrote:

In the research that has been carried out in both the experimental analysis of behavior and applied behavioral analysis, we have not seen a single piece of evidence, a single study, single sentence that would support a conclusion contrary to the following statement: *If you have a behavior that could be changed through the use of aversive contingencies, then it could also be changed through positive contingencies.* [p. 9]

During the week between sessions, Ben called me to let me know he'd found the article interesting. "No punishment is a tough concept for a military man," he'd said. He mentioned that he recently grounded Charlie for cursing. He then said, "These ideas don't come easy for me, but I want to work with you on it—for Charlie's sake."

At the beginning of the next session I learned that Charlie had tantrumed and punched a hole in the kitchen wall in reaction to Ben's grounding him. Charlie listened with poorly contained delight at his father's rendition of the incident. He had done restitution by way of chores and was grounded for three days. According to Ben, Charlie had arrived home from school each day, eager to do his chores. And for the next few days everything had gone well. Yet there was one troubling matter. Ben's Lexus had been scratched during the period when Charlie was grounded. Although there was no direct evidence of Charlie's guilt, he was clearly a suspect. Moreover, it had become a topic of excessive concern for Charlie. Charlie had always liked to talk about the Lexus, wash it, show it to people, and compare it to other cars. Now there was nothing else he talked about as much as the damage to the Lexus.

I asked Charlie directly if he had anything to do with the scratching of the Lexus, which he vehemently denied. I attempted to continue with last week's discussion of the behavioral target sheet, but Charlie kept coming back to the scratches on the Lexus. "I'm really mad that this happened!" he said indignantly. "But I'm even more mad about people thinking I did it. I don't want to get blamed for this."

Both Ben and I assured Charlie that no judgment had been passed on him, but he would not let us get off the topic. However, the more he railed about the injustice that had been done to both the Lexus and himself, the more we suspected that he had done the damage. It seemed that he was caught in a bind between an urge to tell the truth and his fear of the consequences that would result from telling the truth.

At this point I told Charlie that I felt it was important to get this matter settled during the session because it was obviously weighing heavily on him. I asked him to look at me directly and tell me which of the following statements was true:

"*One*: you're upset because you're being blamed for something you didn't do. *Two*: you're upset because you did it, you feel bad, and you can't get it off your mind."

Charlie howled in protest against the latter suggestion, and began to campaign in his own defense. He attempted to elicit promises from his father that he would not get consequences, because there was "no way I'm guilty."

Trying to find an opening, I said, "Charlie, let's make a deal. If you can dig into your memory and remember that you did this, admit it, and take responsibility, I'll try to talk your father into giving you simple restitution with no grounding or other consequences."

Charlie sat up with a start. Even though he made further denials, it was clear he had started thinking things over. There then arose a silent understanding between me and Ben that it was important for Charlie to be able to tell the truth. This was not only about the value of telling the truth for Charlie's sake; it had important ramifications for honesty in their relationship. I felt that Ben was caught between wanting to send "the right message" to his son and his becoming aware that it was Charlie's fear of consequences that was preventing him from being honest.

Ben then said, "Think back, Charlie, are you sure you didn't do it? Remember what I said before. If you can remember that you did it and you can tell me, you'll only get one day of grounding."

"Well, I didn't," Charlie asserted, "and I don't want to get blamed or grounded for something I didn't do!"

I suddenly became aware that during this session Charlie had been extremely focused. There had been a total absence of distracting antics. It felt to me like a good time for a values-based intervention. I turned to Ben and said, "Ben, what do you think about taking the kind of approach that Dr. LaVigna described? How do you feel about making honesty in your relationship with Charlie the most important thing right now?"

Ben took a deep breath and said, "Sounds okay to me."

I turned to Charlie and said, "Charlie, if you can tell us the truth here and now, you won't get consequenced. If you can drum up the courage to be honest, and trust your father to keep his word, no consequences."

Charlie was dumbfounded. "No consequences!" he exclaimed. "You mean no grounding and no restitution either?" We nodded.

"But if Mom hears about this, what will she say?"

We assured Charlie that there would be no consequences from his mother.

Charlie looked down and said, "Well, I *might* have done it, but I'm not sure."

We remained silent as he hedged and then finally stated that he was afraid to tell the truth because he didn't want the consequences. Eventually he said, "Well, maybe I did it." I asked him to make a direct admission and talk about what he was feeling as he was scratching his father's car. He reluctantly talked about his anger and then quickly launched into a barrage of questions, the intent of which was to guarantee him immunity forever for this particular deed. We ended the session on a positive note: Charlie's father was pleased that his son had summoned up the courage to be honest, and Charlie was relieved that he was not going to be punished.

At the next session Ben and Charlie said they had been getting along fairly well, but Ben felt that Charlie had an "attitude problem." He went on to tell me that Charlie had delayed taking his medication, causing him to be late for a business meeting. I asked Charlie if he could tell us what that was about. He squirmed, and said, "What's the difference between a boomerang and a kangaroo?" He then sang a few lines of "The Little Old Lady From Pasadena," and slouched down into his seat. When I suggested a re-enactment in which they would repeat what happened, I was surprised when Charlie jumped up enthusiastically.

When we got to the part of their interaction where Charlie was stalling and staring into space, I asked him what he was feeling. After a number of prompts he admitted that he was angry and finally admitted he knew his father was in a hurry and was getting back at him for a time he had been grounded. I told Charlie that there was nothing wrong with being angry, and that if he could talk about his anger when it came up maybe he wouldn't have to do things that made his relationship with his father more difficult. He nodded thoughtfully, and asked, "Why did the pregnant chicken cross the road?" Clearly, this was enough inward focus for one session. Nevertheless, I felt that Charlie's prior disclosure about scratching the Lexus had made it easier for him this week to tell us the truth about how his behavior was related to being angry with his father.

Ben was still convinced that Charlie needed a way to be monitored until he proved he was capable of mature behavior. I felt that a self-monitoring program was a middle ground that might work for both father and son (see Figure 12–2). With this program Charlie would have to make an honest assessment of his own behavior and talk openly with his father. It gave father and son a common project that benefited them both. There would be no consequences, so that Charlie had nothing to fear or fight against. This structured format brought Charlie and his father together, and provided Charlie with a way to assume greater responsibility and ownership of his behavior.

The self-monitoring program improved Ben and Charlie's relationship greatly, and they led a more or less peaceful coexistence while waiting for the return of the lady of the house. It did not surprise me that when Charlie's mother returned he again made riding his bike to school a major issue. It was almost as if he wanted her to participate in the problem-solving process. He also knew that she would be sympathetic to his cause.

I saw the family together and told Charlie that we needed to talk openly and honestly about his disability. This was painful to him, and he went on at length about how unfair it was that other kids ride their bikes to school, but I reiterated my main point several times that he would have to come to terms with the limitations of his disability. I was surprised that when I spoke about individuals in wheelchairs, those who are deaf and blind, and others with far more severe limitations than his, it made no impression whatsoever on him. "That's different," he said. "I'm not in a wheelchair. I know how to ride a bike, and it's not fair that I can't ride it to school."

I could see that this process was also difficult for Charlie's parents, and I had the feeling that this topic had never been broached directly. But they were courageous, good-hearted people, and although we did not arrive at any easy answers, a great deal of love was expressed in this session. I told them frankly that Charlie's acceptance of his own disability would be greatly affected by the degree to which they had accepted it.

This was yet another encounter for Charlie with the truth. Fortunately, his parents came to understand the importance of coming to terms with the issue of his disability, which they had been struggling with for many years. The end result was that they developed more realistic expectations of Charlie and became more actively involved in long-term planning for his future. They provided opportunities for Charlie to have more freedom in other ways by tapping extended family resources and seeing that he went camping, went to family reunions, and had greater exposure to the world at large. As a result, Charlie had more to talk about with his peers and felt better about himself, and the matter of riding his bike to school faded into the background.

In this case, telling the truth and facing the truth superseded short-term behavioral goals. As Charlie had a supportive environment, he learned to become more honest and deal with his feelings as they arose. His behavior problems decreased, and he was eventually able to leave home and live in a supported living environment with a minimum of supervision.

Figure 12-2

CHARLIE'S SELF-MONITORING FORM

Date: _____

From arriving from school until dinner:
Behavior 1:   Cooperates around the house
                    (cleans room, helps with chores, etc.)

Self Rating	1	2	3	4

Behavior 2:   Positive interactions (no yelling, cursing, lying)

Self Rating	1	2	3	4

Comments: _____

_____

From dinner until bedtime:
Behavior 1:   Cooperates around the house
                    (cleans room, helps with chores, etc.)

Self Rating	1	2	3	4

Behavior 2:   Positive interactions (no yelling, cursing, lying)

Self Rating	1	2	3	4

Comments: _____

_____

Key:
4 = Outstanding   2 = Okay
3 = Good   1 = Will Try Harder

13

WHEN FOUL IS FAIR:

Reinterpreting Negative Behaviors and Engaging the Child's Curiosity and Playfulness

Based on a referral from his case manager with the Department of Children's Services, I went to meet Tim, a 12-year-old from an inner city neighborhood, at the foster home where he'd been living for the past eight months. The social worker had explained that Tim's aggressions had become so severe that both his foster care and school placements were in jeopardy, and he had asked me to do an assessment and make recommendations. Tim's foster mother explained that he was around the corner watching men work. She gave the impression of being overwhelmed by Tim, saying, "We just don't know what to do with him. He gets out of control. I'm afraid to let him go over there by himself, but I'm also afraid to make him stay home with me. He's hit me before when I told him not to do things."

I walked around the corner and found Tim sitting on an old tire, watching a house being demolished. I asked him how he was doing. He said, "Awesome, cool!" I had the impression that he was responding to the sight of a wall collapsing rather than to my question.

I explained to him that his case manager had asked me to come and see how he was doing, also mentioning that I had spoken with his foster mother. He pointed to the workers and said, "This is awesome! They're knocking it down."

He pointed to a truck full of broken pieces of plaster and wood, saying, "They carry it away with that truck. I like the way they smash it. Do you know how to drive those machines, like the big bulldozers? Do you know how to drive them and smash things?"

I told him that I did not know how to drive a bulldozer. He said, "Man, when I grow up, I want to drive a bulldozer or else one of those big, big things with the ball that swings and smashes buildings and stuff."

I asked what else he'd like to do when he grew up.

He said, "Like these guys, with bulldozers or the big ball, to smash things, and not just houses but big buildings, too. And I like race cars, fast race cars, like in the Indianapolis 500. I've seen that on TV. They're fast and I can do that when I grow up. Right?" He gestured as though he held a race car in each hand, driving through the air around him.

As we continued our conversation, Tim picked up a three-foot-long two-by-four that was sticking out from under the fence around the house. I noticed that a rusty nail was sticking out of one end, and I instinctively wanted to reach over and grab it out of his hand, but I held myself back from doing so. He brandished it like a sword at an imaginary foe and then looked at me. He seemed to be waiting for me to reprimand him and try to take this weapon away from him. I suspected that he was accustomed to power struggles with adults.

I said, "Be careful not to hurt yourself with that nail in the end." Given what I'd heard about Tim from his case manager, I was somewhat afraid that he might hurt me. As he continued dueling with an imaginary foe, I asked who he was fighting with.

He said, "Smashing bad guys."

I asked him who those "bad guys" were.

He said, "Like on TV in L.A." Then he looked at me and said, "And also the ones who tell me what to do all the freaking time."

I said "You really don't like people telling you what to do."

He said, "Yeah!" as he lunged forward into space.

We continued talking about his feelings and fantasies, and his brandishing of the "sword" gradually decreased. I asked him about his aggressive episodes, and he said that what had made him mad was other kids teasing him at school and his "fake mom" and "stupid teacher" giving him tasks like homework or chores to do. After about thirty minutes, I told him that I'd be walking back to his house. I asked if he was planning on staying to continue watching the workers.

He said, "I'll come." I then glanced down at the two-by-four in his hand and began walking. Out of the corner of my eye, I saw him glance at the stick, shrug, and throw it over the fence.

Throughout our conversation, I had tried to avoid getting into a power struggle with Tim. I took his voluntarily throwing down his weapon to follow me as a positive sign that he valued empathic, contactful relationship more than his internal world of destructive fantasy.

My assessment of Tim involved a number of discussions with him, his foster parents, and his teacher as well as a **functional analysis**, a review of recent psychological test data, and a review of recent behavioral incident reports from school. Tim's recent negative behaviors included a number of serious aggressive episodes, including one during which he hurt another boy at school by hitting him with a broom handle. He had also been acting up at night, making noise, breaking things, and threatening to run away. And over the past three weeks there had been two incidents of fire starting.

I learned that, although Tim had good verbal skills, he had significant deficits in auditory processing and abstract reasoning, so he often appeared to be higher functioning than he actually was, pretending to understand or be capable of things that were beyond his ability. These disabilities seemed to be a result of neurological problems caused by maternal drug abuse during pregnancy. It was also clear that he had been physically and sexually abused during early childhood, apparently by a number of different men who lived or spent time in his mother's house. He had then also been molested by an older male client in a juvenile hall setting at age 10, when the Department of Children's Services had taken him away from his mother upon her arrest for sale of narcotics.

His first recorded incidents of acting out aggressively were from first and second grade. Apparently, nondisabled peers had teased him for being "stupid" and he'd reacted by fighting with them. From that time on, it appeared that whenever something made Tim angry he would fly into a blind, aggressive rage.

My assessment of Tim's challenging behaviors revealed a few different antecedents and possible functions. In school, teasing by nondisabled peers led to incidents of his acting out to impress his peers as well as to more rare but severe incidents of aggression toward peers. Once Tim entered these states of aggressive rage, he had a very hard time calming down, and so these were of particular concern to his teacher. He also sometimes became aggressive when faced with directives from his foster parents or teacher to perform tasks such as math assignments or cleaning his bedroom. His difficulties at night seemed to be related to his having difficulty sleeping, though he was unwilling to discuss his sleep problems with me or his foster parents. The two incidents of Tim's starting fires seemed to be the result of an interest he had developed in magnifying glasses, which he had learned about at school. In the first incident, he had taken a magnifying glass that he had been using in class outside during recess and set a piece of paper on fire. In the second, he had found a magnifying glass in a drawer at home and had set a pile of trash that he had taken from a garbage can on fire; his foster mother had found him with his small fire and put it out but had been extremely concerned because the flames were just outside the garage, which was made of wood and contained numerous flammable liquids.

Although Tim clearly had a difficult time trusting others, he had seemed to develop positive bonds particularly with his foster mother and his female teacher. Based on this, everyone had hoped for a gradual decrease in his challenging behaviors, and they were very upset by his current behavior problems.

As I reflected on Tim's case, I was reminded of an adult female client who had a personal history of abuse, neglect, and behavioral acting out similar to Tim's. She had been placed in a number of campus-based facilities with highly structured behavioral programs. These programs had succeeded in eliminating these behaviors, and she had become capable of living in an assisted living apartment program and holding two part-time jobs. However, she was continually plagued by intense feelings of anxiety, leading to a variety of somatic complaints including migraine headaches and gastrointestinal distress. Psychotherapy revealed that the highly structured behavioral programs she had been in had created a highly compliant persona or, in D. W. Winnicott's (1986) terms, a "false self" capable of basic superficial social and self-care functions but incapable of meaningful interpersonal relationships, creativity, or joy. In the absence of any genuine friendships or personal interests, her mental life was taken up with continuous worry about her health and about the minutiae of her daily routine.

So, in developing a treatment plan, I was mindful of the fact that while decreasing Tim's dangerous behaviors was essential, helping him to work through some of the underlying causes of these behaviors was equally important. D. W. Winnicott (1986) has been very helpful in pointing out that severely challenging or antisocial behaviors in a child who has been subject to severe deprivations or abuse can actually be a positive sign. Severe neglect and abuse can easily lead a child to simply give up on connecting with others; overwhelmed by fear and anxiety, he may lock his capacities for love and creativity away inside of himself. Seemingly antisocial behaviors can be seen as a sign that the child is trying to connect, trying to work through the traumas and deprivations that have injured him.

Winnicott (1992) further explains that children develop many of their capacities for positive relationships, trust, and creativity during early experiences of play. The presence of loving adults is essential at this stage for the child's developing sense of confidence in the outer environment and in his inner potential. In Tim's case, though, his early experiences of play had been disturbed by an emotionally absent mother and by abusive intrusions. Winnicott says that "exploitation of this area leads to a pathological condition in which the individual is cluttered up with persecutory fears" (p. 103). As I got to know Tim better, I realized that persecutory fears of this kind were what made it so difficult for him to sleep, causing his disruptive nighttime behaviors. Memories of his abuse and neglect would appear as horrific monsters in Tim's dreams and fantasies. This also explained Tim's need to "smash" bad guys and giant buildings in his fantasy play. These were attempts to assert the control that he did not have during his abusive early childhood and to master these internalized demons of his dreams.

I met with Tim's foster parents and teacher to discuss my observations. I emphasized my belief that Tim's current behavior problems pointed to *success* rather than failure on their part. They had succeeded in allowing Tim to feel more safe and comfortable than he had in years. This had moved him, bringing up his deep desire for loving and contact. But his severely abusive past had taught him well that love and trust were extremely dangerous, so some of his acting out reflected his inner conflicts between his desire to trust and his fears. We discussed how his aggression was also a way of testing others' love and hope for him. His foster mother said, "It's like he's trying to prove he's bad and no one can love him, but he's so hungry for love." I was impressed by both of his foster parents' commitment to his well-being despite his behavioral problems.

Regarding Tim's treatment plan, we decided to use **covert reinforcement** to teach him specific positive ways of reacting when someone teased him or asked him to do a nonpreferred task. I felt that this method would be helpful because, while teaching replacement behaviors, it would also provide a structured format for his foster parents to spend time with him, engaging his imagination in a positive way. A behavioral contract for using the reactions taught in his covert reinforcement sequences rather then becoming aggressive was also created.

For the reasons discussed above, I also recommended play therapy for Tim. In addition to weekly meetings with a therapist, though, his foster parents purchased a number of toys specifically for Tim to express himself through play. These included bulldozers and cranes as well as Legos, Lincoln Logs, and other materials for building. His foster mother agreed that each evening the two of them would have 30–45 minutes of "special playtime," when she would be with him as he expressed himself through play. The idea here was that he have a safe, regular time and place to express destructive or creative impulses within the presence and understanding of someone who cared for him. The foster mother agreed that she would not judge his actions during these times but would simply focus on being with him in an empathic way.

Also, given that Tim had recently expressed an interest in science at school, his foster father, who worked as an engineer, agreed to purchase a number of items for a science kit, including a microscope and a small inexpensive telescope. He agreed that he would spend time each week with Tim looking at the night sky or finding things in their local environment to look at through the microscope. Our hope was to engage his creativity and interest in a positive way while trying to decrease potentially dangerous play such as his fire starting using magnifying glasses.

To address his acting out at night, Tim's foster parents bought him a night light and began reading him soothing stories before bed each night. They also told him that if he was feeling afraid, then instead of acting out he could just come and talk with them.

Over the next few months, Tim's behaviors generally improved. His difficulties at night disappeared almost immediately once his foster parents were able to reframe these as an issue of *safety* rather than one of *control*. His foster parents also reported that he very much enjoyed having his "special playtime" and the opportunities to engage in scientific explorations with his foster father. There were no more incidents of fire starting.

Although Tim was still short-tempered at times—particularly when teased by peers—both his teacher and his foster parents agreed that within two months they had reached a level at which they were tolerable.

When faced with a child exhibiting dangerous or antisocial behaviors, there are always a number of options in how we will work with that child. It is important to be aware of both the benefits and side effects that any given approach may be likely to lead to. Creativity, curiosity, and imagination are, naturally, essential to psychological health and a good quality of life. Often, these qualities are neglected when plans are developed for working with developmentally disabled children. I have found that engaging these positive psychological capacities as part of one's approach to a child—even, or perhaps especially, a child exhibiting antisocial tendencies—can be extremely useful in helping the child to progress and is much less likely to produce negative side effects than approaches that ignore or work against these tendencies.

14

YOUR SPACE BUBBLE AND MINE:

Working with Boundaries and Self–Other Differentiation

I received a call from a family who wanted to discuss the pros and cons of placing their daughter, Karen, in a group home. They loved her very much, but she had frequent tantrums leading to property destruction and would often attack them when they least expected it. They had spent the last ten years of their life trying to accommodate her moods and cope with her behavior. They walked around the house on eggshells, dreading the next angry outbreak.

At our first session the mother had a need to ventilate considerable pent-up anger about Karen's special education teacher, who, she believed, did not understand her daughter and how to work effectively with her. The father listened patiently, minimizing the problems we were discussing whenever he had a chance to speak. Karen was the apple of her father's eye, and he wanted her to stay at home. The mother reminded him that since the onset of menstruation Karen's behavior had gotten completely out of hand. Moreover their 10-year-old son was not getting the energy and attention he needed. By the end of the session they both agreed that they could not cope with Karen in her current state, but that it would break their hearts to see her leave home.

I suggested that they put their decision about placing Karen in a group home on hold until I had a chance to observe Karen at school and make treatment recommendations. I agreed to monitor behavioral reports, meet with Karen, confer with teachers, and work with the entire family if needed.

Karen was a tall and sturdily built 13-year-old with dark hair and a ruddy complexion. She had a diagnosis of **Pervasive Developmental Disorder** NOS and Moderate Mental Retardation. When I visited her classroom she appeared to be fun-loving and playful, as she giggled and joked with her classmates. Due to expressive speech impairments she had difficulty forming complete sentences, but was able to communicate her wants and needs fairly well.

What struck me most from the outset was that Karen could not separate herself from the problems of others. If a peer in her classroom was crying or having an argument, Karen immediately became upset and began banging her head. It seemed as if the moods and emotions of others reverberated physically through Karen. I took particular note of the fact that, if a peer was upset, Karen would substitute her name for that of the peer. She would say "Karen angry" and become agitated, or "Karen sad" and begin to cry in situations that had nothing do with her personally. There was at times no **boundary** between herself and others. I hypothesized that Karen had not yet resolved the poor self–other differentiation of what Mahler (1968) calls the *symbiotic* phase of psychosocial development. During this phase, the child experiences "unpleasurable events as encompassing its entire self and entire world" (Hamilton 1988, p. 40). As many behavioral programs had been tried with little success, I began to look at Karen's tantrums in terms of her needing to more fully differentiate herself from others and establish better boundaries. She needed to learn to more effectively regulate what she allowed into her own personal circle of experience, so she could be better able to distinguish what belonged to her from what belonged to others.

Due to the severity of Karen's tantrums at school, she was assigned a school psychologist named Daniel to do what in California is called a Hughes Bill behavioral intervention plan. The Hughes Bill is a piece of legislation that mandates special education programs to provide (among other things) a formal assessment, including functional analysis and positive intervention plan to address behaviors that pose a danger to self and others. At the family's request, it was decided that I would work collaboratively with Daniel on Karen's intervention plan. I had worked with him previously on a number of other cases, and so when we heard about a Hughes Bill seminar in Los Angeles led by Dr. Menzes, a Positive Programming specialist, we decided to do a case presentation together.

When we arrived I was surprised to learn this was a mandated seminar and that about thirty school psychologists had been obliged to attend. There was an air of resentment, which was immediately directed toward the unfortunate seminar leader, Dr. Menzes.

Things went from bad to worse very quickly because Dr. Menzes thought it was a propos to the concept of positive reinforcement to throw candies at the participants who gave good answers to his questions. "What is your understanding of a functional analysis?" he asked a psychologist who was clearly his senior, and responded to the answer with a hearty, "*Very good!*" and threw him a pop tart. There was an immediate uproar, and after several such incidents there was nearly a mutiny. For me, it was quite entertaining to witness a situation in which a group of behavior specialists were exhibiting a signficant "behavioral problem." After lunch, the matronly school district representative who had taken the roll call announced that the completion of the seminar with full participation was a condition of employment—and that settled that. Definitely *not* a positive programming type of intervention.

By the time it was our turn to present I had lost my enthusiasm. It was as if I had been conscripted into the group mood. The other participants had lapsed into a kind of passive-aggressive sullenness, and I found myself particularly disgruntled with Dr. Menzes's insistence that the function or communicative intent of *all* problematic behavior can be accounted for by *attention seeking, avoidance, getting/obtaining, and self-stimulation.* I was familiar with the Durand functional analysis data collection sheet he was using, and had found it difficult to apply in most settings. Besides, the implied assumptions about the dynamics of human behavior were painfully superficial.

Feeling this way, I thought it would be best to let Daniel present the more conventional aspects of the intervention plan, and follow up with a food-for-thought addendum. However, Daniel had staunchly joined the ranks of the disaffected as a physically present nonparticipant, and turned the presentation over to me.

I started off with the known **antecedents** of Karen's tantrum behavior, which included class members leaving the room for appointments (Karen wanted to go with them), transitions to another classroom or physical locale, and individual peer problems and interpersonal problems between peers.

I explained that the conventional categories of the communicative intent of behaviors did not adequately explain Karen's problems. She clearly had a *weak self–other boundary*. She would feel or take on almost any tension or conflict between others in her classroom. She was not trying to attract attention, get or avoid anything, or stimulate herself. She was able to meet her need for attention by way of signaling gestures, acting coy, and giggling. She escalated into an acute state of stress, though, whenever there were individual tensions or interpersonal problems nearby. Due to her expressive speech deficit, she was unable to resolve this by talking about what and how she felt. I presented the following boundary exercises, which could be implemented by teachers and parents.

INTERPERSONAL BOUNDARY EXERCISES

1. Self–other differentiation with puppets and dolls.

One puppet is called Karen and the other puppet is Karen's friend Sally. A line is drawn with chalk on the table separating them. The teacher points to Sally and makes a statement about Sally's feelings or behavior. Then Karen makes a behavior and feeling statement about Sally. It is emphasized with "This is Sally's behavior / Sally's feeling—*not Karen's*!"

2. I Feel, You Feel, game.

Karen and teacher take turns pointing to themselves and each other, making *I* statements and *you* statements.

3. Space-Bubble Boundary exercise.

Karen draws a circle around herself on the floor and the teacher comes close to the edge and retreats, observing Karen's responses and giving feedback. This can also be done with puppets and stuffed animals. Karen is asked what it feels like when the animal goes through the perimeter of her space bubble and is in the circle when she doesn't want it in.

4. Go-Go Stop! Boundary game.

Teacher draws a line with chalk or uses colored yarn to indicate a boundary and then asks Karen to approach. She says *Stop* when Karen touches the line. She then says, "You touched the edge of my *space bubble.*" After doing this 5–10 times, it's Karen's turn. *Stop* can also be conveyed by a word, rasing your hand, or with a stop sign.

I explained to the seminar participants that personal boundaries often need to be externalized for the disabled (as well as other client populations) so that they can have a physical experience of self located in space, clearly demarcated from another person. I enlisted several volunteers for the above exercises, and by the time we were done the atmosphere in the room had perked up. Dr. Menzes was so relieved that he admitted through clenched teeth that this approach "might have some merit."

A week later I had a meeting with Karen's parents and teacher to present these interventions for their use. Daniel also designed a **positive reinforcement** schedule to complement and support the boundary work.

I continued meeting with the family to help them through their own process of establishing healthier boundaries in the home, so that they could get their own needs met while still caring for Karen. It took several months to help Karen's mother work through guilt feelings she had about her daughter's condition, and she came to accept the fact that Karen's condition was not caused by anything she had done or not done. She realized that she needed to create more personal space for herself, and so she took on a part-time job and began going out more. When her energy and attention were absorbed in ways that gave her a life beyond the realm of Karen's behavioral problems, she had more to give to her son, and the time she spent with Karen was more defined and satisfying.

Karen's mother and father began to re-create their relationship by scheduling time together, having fun, and tapping other resources such as family members and church volunteers to help out with Karen. As the family system itself developed better boundaries, everyone felt better about themselves and each other. Karen's behavior at home improved greatly, and this was as much a response to increased family happiness as it was to the intervention plan that was implemented.

Karen eventually learned how to walk away from situations that she knew she could not tolerate. Although she was not always able to cope with what came into her "space bubble," she learned to better anticipate the situations that would be problematic and to cope with them without becoming aggressive. Through her parents' positive modeling and her ongoing participation in boundary exercises, her ability to differentiate others' feeling from her own and take care of her own needs improved greatly.

Good boundaries make for good relationships in all our interpersonal endeavors. Each of us has the right to regulate what comes into our own "space bubble." And this being so, it behooves us to respect what others allow or disallow to come into theirs. Individuals with disabilities certainly face special challenges in communicating how much closeness and distance are acceptable, but boundary awareness is often the key to both understanding and meeting individual and family needs in the delicate interplay of self–other differentiation and interpersonal connectedness.

15

THE TRIALS OF TOILET TRAINING:

Behavioral, Developmental, and Practical Considerations

A challenging case involving the toilet training of an 11-year-old autistic boy taught me a good deal about how the integration of clinical understanding, a practical intervention, and the patient dedication of caregivers is essential to successful treatment. This boy, whose name was David, had lived at home until two months before his eleventh birthday, and his parents had shown remarkable dedication to his development and well-being. They had gone to scores of workshops and conferences on the treatment of autism and had struggled to implement numerous treatment modalities in their home over the past decade. They had tried various combinations of sensory-motor therapy, behavioral therapy, auditory integration training, as well as dietary and vitamin regimens. David had extremely limited, highly echolalic speech, and his parents had tried a number of augmentative communication strategies including sign language, picture pointing, and facilitated communication.

Regarding his toileting problems, David's parents still had the documentation from a number of toileting schedules that they had tried. They reported that he had twice gone through periods of being *habit trained*—periods during which he would use the bathroom successfully so long as he was kept on a very strict schedule, with an adult taking him to the toilet every 30–45 minutes. However, keeping to that schedule over the course of months was extremely difficult, and slippage quickly led to increases in David's accidents. David had never reached the point of using the bathroom independently with any consistency, and when I was first asked to consult on this case, he was wearing pull-up diapers and was on a schedule of being taken to the toilet once every hour. David was having an average of one accident involving defecation and two accidents involving urination per day. Particularly after incidents of defecation, if they were not noticed immediately, David would smear feces on himself and on his bed or a couch. On a number of occasions, he had covered himself with a blanket and then smeared feces on both his own face and the inside of the blanket. During an interview about these behaviors, his parents noted that he seemed to enjoy both playing with and smelling his own feces.

David's father's work as a salesman was causing him to be out of town more frequently than the family had been accustomed to, and although his mother's part-time work at a bank allowed her to be home with him after school, she was finding it increasingly difficult to deal with his toileting problems, particularly during summers and holidays when school was not in session. The teachers in his special education classroom were also frustrated with their inability to successfully toilet train David.

So the family was pleased when they were able to find a placement in a local ten-bed group home. They would continue to be able to see him as often as they liked and he would be able to remain in his current classroom, but David would have a team of staff to implement a toileting program for him, and his parents would be freed from having to clean him two to three times per day. When David was accepted into this group home, his parents called me to discuss his toilet training program. They told me the history of their attempts to toilet train him and explained that the group home to which he would be moving had not previously done toilet training but was expressing a willingness to implement an appropriate behavioral program. They asked me if I would be willing to make recommendations and provide training to the group home staff.

After a fairly brief assessment involving a few sessions of direct observation, a review of the available data, and interviews with David's parents, teachers, and new staff, I recommended that the toileting program designed for children with autism by Dr. Ivar Lovaas be used with David. I recommended this program because it was appropriate to David's diagnosis and functioning level and because it provides an effective alternative to the use of scheduled trips to the toilet, which had not been effective for David. In essence, Dr. Lovaas's method involves having the child initially sit on the toilet for long periods of time in order to increase his familiarity with being on the toilet and to ensure that he will have a number of successes (and no or very few accidents). Successes are strongly reinforced with praise, rewards, and time away from the toilet. Ordinarily, time on the toilet decreases quickly over the first few days as the child learns to understand and appreciate successful use of the toilet.

I believed that David's strong interest in smelling and playing with his feces was also important to consider. In his discussion of the **anal stage** of psychosexual development, Freud (1969) and Miller (1983) noted that pre-toilet–trained children gain sensual pleasure through defecation and feces. Based on past success with other autistic clients, I suggested that part of David's program be that he have regular access to modeling clay as well as to a variety of perfumes and aromatherapy scents. The idea here was to give him opportunities to get his sensory desires met while also, in a sense, teaching him to sublimate these desires into more socially acceptable outlets.

I shared these recommendations with the group home manager and suggested that they hire a young woman I knew who had a good deal of experience with Dr. Lovaas's toileting program to train the staff and help them during the first few days of implementing the program.

After this, I didn't hear anything further about David's case for a couple of months; then his parents called me again. They told me that the toileting program had not worked and that the group home's supervisor wanted to discharge David. They were very upset, as his toileting problems had not improved at all, and his mother had recently begun working full time. They asked me to see if there were anything else that could be done.

I visited the group home the following evening in order to speak with the staff who had been working with David about what had happened. When I explained who I was to the staff member who was working with David that night, he was very happy to talk with me. He explained that it had taken over a month for the group home to get staffing in place and to hire the consultant I had suggested in order to begin implementing the suggested toileting program. During those five weeks, David had continued to have very frequent accidents and to smear feces. The staff, who were unfamiliar with this behavior, had become extremely frustrated with David and, despite their efforts to keep things clean, a number of the staff and other clients had become ill, which they attributed to David's unclean behaviors. By the time the recommended toilet program was ready to be implemented, a significant number of the staff working with David felt that he was inappropriately placed and should be discharged.

Then the consultant I had recommended had come in and had taught them the technical skills involved in the suggested method. I spoke with her, and she told me that she had observed a number of different staff implementing the toileting program over a period of three days, and that they were implementing it correctly. Over the course of my conversation with her, though, it became clear that, beneath the smiles and apparent technical compliance with the prescribed program, she had detected some frustration and even anger on the part of the staff at having to work with David. If she had picked up on this, I felt confident that David had as well. Although people with autism generally have difficulty understanding the subtler points of social interactions, it has been my observation that they are sometimes almost hyperaware of whether others' body language and energetic expression toward them is accepting or rejecting. In David's case, I suspected that feelings of rejection associated with being away from home for the first time combined with his feeling rejected by staff was leading to feelings of anger and a lack of willingness to cooperate with the toileting program.

I spoke about this with David's parents and suggested that they consider bringing him home and having a team of consultants work with them in the home to try implementing the toileting program there. They feared, though, that if they took him home he would lose his placement in the group home and that they then might be unable to manage him at home. I agreed to meet with the parents, the group home manager, and the group home staff all together to discuss what was to be done with David. I encouraged the staff to express themselves openly about their work with David in this setting, as frank discussion is a necessary step toward getting at negative feelings that might otherwise be acted out with the client. When the group home manager agreed not to consequence the staff for being honest, and the parents expressed an openness to hearing what was really going on, the staff's feelings of frustration and anger at having to clean up urine and feces on a daily basis quickly surfaced. They felt that this had not been part of their job expectations when they were hired, and they resented this change. Although direct care staff working with developmentally disabled children often find themselves in some of the most difficult situations that exist in the health care field, they are very rarely given an opportunity to air or discuss their feelings about this. Often, a culture is created in which those expressing such feelings are made to feel guilty for thinking badly of someone with a disability. I have found, though, that honesty within an atmosphere of safety and professionalism is most effective in dealing with these issues.

After this group meeting, I met privately with the group home manager and suggested that she tell her staff that no one was going to be forced to work with David, but that she was looking for volunteers to work as many hours per week with him as felt comfortable to them. She did so, and found that beneath their feelings of frustration and anger, a number of staff had developed a positive attachment to David. Three of these staff each volunteered to spend twelve of their forty hours per week working with David. They were particularly interested in attempting the toileting program again, as they very much wanted to see him succeed. The manager herself then offered to work two four-hour shifts per week on line with David because she too wanted to see the program succeed and because she felt that she should not ask others to implement something that she would not do herself. She decided to rehire the consultant I had suggested for additional hours during their next attempt with the toileting program.

I met with this group of staff and reviewed the specifics of Dr. Lovaas's program to be sure that they all understood just how it was to be implemented. We also had a useful discussion about how challenging it can be to toilet train someone David's age with a disability. Psychologists since Freud have noted that toilet training involves a struggle between the child's desire for autonomy and adults' practical need to introduce control into the child's life. As one developmental psychologist (Miller 1983) put it, "Their desire for immediate gratification is frustrated. In a small but momentous way, children enter into conflict with authoritarian adult society" (p. 133). A child like David who had limited ability to control other aspects of his life and who has gone longer than other children in not being toilet trained can present a formidable obstacle to those working with him. What occurs is a battle for control in the arena of the bathroom as well as within the child, who is intent on asserting his autonomy. Therefore, it is important for caregivers to remain firm in their resolve, while also being playful and engaging with the child, so that the results will be cooperation and growth rather than resentment or rigidity.

Within a few days, they again began implementing the prescribed toileting program. This time it was very successful. David's time on the toilet quickly decreased as his successes increased. During breaks, he seemed to particularly enjoy the stronger aromatherapy scents he had been bought. Within one week, David was only being reminded to use the bathroom every two and one-half hours, and he had used the bathroom independently on a number of occasions. I asked the consultant who had been spending a considerable amount of time at the group home what had changed. She said that there had been no changes in the behavioral program itself, but that everyone's attitude now seemed much more positive. Staff were laughing with David, and cheering with great enthusiasm when he went successfully in the toilet.

Four months later, I again visited this group home in my work with another client. I was told that they had gone through a few difficult weeks, when David had briefly reverted to previous behaviors, but the team's brief but quick reimplementation of the previously successful program had quickly brought this under control. He was now using the bathroom independently. He had not had an accident involving defecation in over a month, and he was only having accidents involving urination once every two to three weeks, primarily when he forgot to use the bathroom before going to an unfamiliar setting and then was unable to locate a bathroom or ask where one was in time to avoid the accident. They were working with him on using a small card that he carried in his pocket with a picture of a toilet on it that he could use to ask staff where the nearest bathroom was in such settings. I was told that his parents were also very pleased and were considering having him come to live at home again.

16

AN ACCEPTANCE OF REALITY:

Jungian Reflections in Psychotherapy with a Young Psychotic Man

Bill Marks was a good-looking, engaging, energetic 21-year-old male. His initial presentation contrasted with a long and complex clinical history. Since early childhood, he had had severe attentional difficulties and intrusive hallucinations that had, during his adolescence, crystalized into a number of delusions, such as a belief that demons or aliens were out to get him and, most recently, a belief that he was a physician. The extent to which Bill was developmentally disabled was not entirely clear. Nevertheless, the symptoms mentioned above in combination with learning disabilities had led him to be placed in special education classrooms with developmentally disabled peers. Since the age of 17, he had been living in a group home for dually diagnosed males, where his parents visited him frequently.

I was asked to see Bill for 15 to 25 sessions of counseling and to make treatment recommendations to his group home staff. At that time, he seemed to be suffering from a depression that had intensified his psychotic symptoms over the past couple of months. I was also asked to talk with him about his plans for the future, as his current funding source would be discontinued in nine months, on his twenty-second birthday, and he had thus far been unwilling to talk with his family or social worker about realistic future plans.

After my second session with Bill, I was asked to come out to his group home to sit in on a psychiatric medication evaluation with a new psychiatrist who had been assigned to him by the county mental health agency. I arrived at Bill's group home at the appointed time and was directed to the staff office. Bill was sitting on a chair outside of the office. I immediately noticed that he was well dressed, wearing a white dress shirt, a navy blue sports coat, and a red tie.

After we had greeted, I said, "Bill, you look very nice today."

He said, "I have to dress up like this."

I asked why and he said, "Because of my position."

I asked what position he was referring to, and he raised his eyebrows and laughed quietly.

Soon, the door opened and another young man walked out. I walked in and introduced myself to the psychiatrist, who seemed to be in her early forties and was wearing beige slacks and a light blue blouse. Bill walked in behind me and sat on a wooden chair. The psychiatrist said, "Hello, Bill. I'm Doctor Kotsubei."

Bill smiled and said, "Hello, I'm Doctor Marks."

"Are you Bill Marks?" she asked, looking a bit uncomfortable.

"Doctor," he answered.

Dr. Kotsubei sighed and then said, "Bill, I'm your psychiatrist. Your mother and your staff here have asked me to meet with you to discuss your medications. We want to see if they're helping you. Okay?"

Bill said, "Of course, I know about medications."

Dr. Kotsubei asked, "Have the medications you've been taking been helping you?"

Bill said, "They're very good. I prescribe them for lots of people. I have to be careful of the side effects, though."

Dr. Kotsubei asked, "Have you been experiencing side effects?"

Bill answered, "No, but my patients did, some of them. So I took them off it."

Dr. Kotsubei asked, "But have you experienced side effects yourself?"

Bill sighed impatiently. "No, them. Not me."

Dr. Kotsubei paused, seemingly uncertain how to proceed. She looked at Bill intently and said, "Listen, Bill, I need to ask you something important. Can you look at me?" She paused again, and he looked at her. Then, slowly and deliberately, she said, "Your last doctor prescribed these medications to help you. At that time you were hearing voices. Do you remember?"

Bill looked a bit uncertain, but he nodded in assent. Dr. Kotsubei continued, "Now, I want to make sure that they're helping you. So now tell me, are you still hearing voices?"

There was a pause. Dr. Kotsubei leaned back, waiting for Bill's answer. Bill leaned forward and squinted as if thinking hard about her question. In the silence, I heard what sounded like a television game show playing in a resident's room across the hall.

Bill nodded, smiled, and leaned back. "Yes. I do hear voices. It's 'Wheel of Fortune.'" Then he leaned forward again with a look of concern; "Dr. Kotsu, can't you hear Vanna White?"

Dr. Kotsubei raised her hand to her head and sighed.

After the medication evaluation was over, I met with Dr. Kotsubei briefly to discuss Bill's condition. She informed me that Bill had received a number of comprehensive neurological assessments over the years and that numerous medications had been tried to control his psychotic symptoms. He was currently on Clozaril, which had brought about some improvement in the intensity and frequency of his auditory hallucinations but had not significantly affected his delusional beliefs.

Dr. Kotsubei also mentioned that, although she was new to Bill's case, she had already received three phone calls from Bill's parents asking her to change his psychotropic medications. Based on the recommendations generated during his most recent neuropsychiatric assessment, his medication history, and his current condition, she felt that a medication change would probably not be helpful. Though neither of us had had extensive contact with Bill's parents, we shared the initial impression that they were very troubled by their son's psychiatric problems and that, despite years of disappointment, they were hoping that Dr. Kotsubei or I might somehow help find a cure for their son.

Although Bill was an adult, his parents were very much involved in his daily life, and they had limited legal conservatorship. I decided to have a meeting with them to discuss the treatment goals of my work with Bill and how I might be helpful in working with him on realistic plans for his future. During our phone conversation to set up this meeting, Bill's father emphasized his belief that Bill's disabling condition should not limit his future opportunities. He said, "I have great hopes that with new medications and your help, many, many things will be possible for Bill." Although I have always felt strongly that people with disabilities should be given as many opportunities as possible, I wondered whether unrealistic expectations might not be part of the problem here.

In our early sessions, when I brought up his plans for the future, Bill became quite anxious, and his delusional talk about being a great surgeon or psychiatrist increased. I began wondering whether this specific delusion didn't partially serve as a defense against his own and his family's disappointment with the limitations that his disability placed on him. Both Bill and his father had mentioned that Bill's two older brothers were well educated and very successful. I wondered whether the family wasn't having difficulty facing the fact that it was extremely unlikely that Bill would live up to the family's standards.

Before the session with Bill's parents, I was reminded of a case study I had read regarding a client of C. G. Jung's (McGuire 1981). The mother of a young man with schizophrenia named Jobic had traveled from her home in America to consult with Jung in Zurich. For years, she had been searching desperately for a cure to her son's condition. Jung apparently helped this woman very profoundly by explaining to her that her son's condition was simply incurable, and so spending time seeking a cure exacerbated their difficulties. The woman later wrote that, while Jung helped her to understand and *accept* her son's incurable psychiatric condition, "Jung on the other hand took Jobic's pure, beautiful side and brought it out into a complete, radiant, conquering thing" (McGuire 1981, p. 186). Jung helped her to see the creative, genuinely human, ultimately spiritual side of her son's personality. While coming to accept her son's condition, she also gained a capacity for connecting with him in a deeper and more accepting way than she had been able to previously, while focused on seeking a cure.

During our meeting, I talked with Bill's parents about my conversation with Dr. Kotsubei regarding Bill's medications. They told me that they had read about cases of people recovering from schizophrenia and that they did not want to give up hope that this could happen for their son. I explained that, while it sounded like Bill had made considerable progress over the years, when a psychotic disorder has had an early onset, as in Bill's case, a complete cure was extremely unusual. I also mentioned that both the experts at the neuropsychiatric institute and Bill's previous and current psychiatrists felt that his current medication regime was appropriate.

Mr. and Mrs. Marks were intelligent people, and they were able to openly discuss their desire that Bill have as full a life as their other sons. I explained that if we were going to help Bill with realistic options for his future, we also had to ground ourselves in a realistic assessment of his strengths and weaknesses. I said, "Despite Bill's neurological difficulties, I feel strongly that he is also basically a good, loving person."

When I said this, Mrs. Marks sighed. She said, "Yes. You should see him at church. How he loves the choir. Though his mind plays tricks on him, his heart, deep down, is a heart of gold."

We all resolved that in order to help Bill through this difficult period, it would be best for everyone to emphasize realistic short-term plans rather than more speculative long-term hopes for a cure. This implied an acceptance of his current limitations, with a focus of building on his current strengths and interests.

In my own work with Bill, I recognized that it was very important to create an atmosphere of safety and acceptance while striving to be clear about the meanings of words and concepts used. For example, in Bill's conversation with Dr. Kotsubei, it was not clear that he fully understood what *side effects* were, and he did not seem to share her understanding of what *hearing voices* meant. It is all too common in working with those with dual diagnoses for misunderstandings of the meanings of words and concepts to waylay effective communication. I recently spoke with a colleague who had a client report to her that she had been raped by a caregiver. This colleague was wise to check with the client regarding what she understood "rape" to mean. As it turned out, the caregiver had made the client do her homework rather than going on a drive in the van. The client had said, "He made me do something I didn't want to! Ain't that rape?" Being sure that a client understands terms that you are using, and that you understand the sometimes unique ways in which they use language, given their learning disabilities and psychiatric problems, is essential.

In my ongoing conversations with Bill, I made it a point to explain my meaning when I used a new term and asked him to be as explicit as possible. Over time, it not only helped us to better understand each other but also gave him the positive message that I truly wished to understand him—a message that many with developmental disabilities and/or psychotic disorders may receive far too rarely.

Perhaps the most significant aspect of my approach to Bill was again based on an insight from Jung (1961). Early in his career, Jung spent years working with schizophrenic adults. Throughout his career, Jung always emphasized accepting the **psychic reality** of the patient. In his work with psychotic people, rather than trying to challenge their delusional beliefs, he developed his own capacity to empathically relate with the strange psychic worlds in which they lived. This is not an approach that will lead to a cure for the psychotic condition, but being able to relate in a genuine and empathic way to the patient's psychic reality can serve as a foundation for helping him to live in that world more effectively and to build bridges between that world and the social reality we share.

For example, with Bill, when the subject of impending changes in his living situation came up, so did his belief that aliens were out to get him. When this happened, I found that the most effective thing that I could do was to reflect that I could hear the anxiety and fear that he was feeling. If I directly tried to link this fear to his outer circumstances rather than to aliens, this led to resistance on his part, but when I simply stuck with empathically relating to his feelings, this seemed to be helpful in the moment, and he was eventually able to note that his feelings about aliens and those about the upcoming life changes were similar.

In one of our sessions, as we spoke about his interest in attending church, Bill came up with an innovative way of dealing with his fears of aliens and demons. Bill realized that he generally felt good in church and that he felt particularly safe and happy when he heard gospel songs or readings from the psalms. Bill was able to get a tape made of his church choir when they were singing some of his favorite songs, and his minister kindly offered to read some of Bill's favorite psalms onto another tape. Bill found that, when he was feeling anxious or afraid, listening to these tapes was helpful. Playing them low in the background during some sessions helped us to discuss his plans for the future without his becoming overwhelmed by delusional fears.

I also found that it was important not to challenge Bill's belief that he was a physician. Such challenges only led to resistance and to suspicion on his part. I did not agree with such assertions but instead listened for what was healthy and potentially helpful for him within or beneath this psychotic defense.

When he would bring up his responsibilities as a physician, I might react by saying something like, "I can hear how you feel responsible for helping others and yourself. It doesn't sound easy." Then I might ask him for specific suggestions about how someone might deal with a challenging situation that he himself was actually facing. For example, I asked him what he thought someone who was feeling depressed might do to help himself. He replied, "Well, I would prescribe more exercise. And going to the park. Also eating good foods." I would write down what he had "prescribed" and then give him a copy of what I'd written. Gradually, though not always consistently, he tried to implement a number of these prescriptions for himself.

I spoke with Bill's family and group home staff about how his "doctor talk" reflected a desire to feel significant and to be able to help others. Seeking additional opportunities for him to take on significant roles, the group home staff had him take on a mentoring role for new residents, "showing them the ropes." His family arranged for him to do some volunteer work at the church. While this certainly did not cure Bill's psychotic disorder, it did improve his self-esteem. Over the months that I worked with him his depression lifted and he became more able to express—in his own unique ways—the positive sides of his personality.

As we finished our work together, Bill and his family decided that he would move into his own apartment a few miles from his parents' home with a live-in aide to help with tasks such as cooking and bill paying. Bill would be able to have regular visits with his family. He also registered in a local job training program, and continued with his volunteer work at the church.

Although it is important not to reinforce delusional beliefs, uncovering real needs that the content of these beliefs may hold can be useful in understanding and working with clients with psychotic disorders. In Bill's case, although he obviously never did become a physician, he was ultimately able to prescribe useful elements of his own treatment.

17

NOBODY CAN TELL ME WHAT TO DO:

Working with the Rosenberg IBP Character Style Model

The trend toward mental health agencies providing wrap-around support services in the community led me out of the office and into the home of a worried family whose dually diagnosed 16-year-old son simply refused to leave his room to participate in therapy or other suggested activities. The referring agency had given me an incomplete file with an outdated DSM diagnosis that listed Borderline Intellectual Functioning / Rule-Out Organic Mental Disorder. The case manager told me that this case was essentially that of a severely aggressive adolescent who went to school but would not do anything else. Both parents were very nervous about the initial visit, as Steve had a long history of punching people in the face without warning.

A review of the file indicated that many behavioral programs had been tried over the years, but Steve's behavior continued to be explosive and unpredictable, most recently involving property damage at school. I had a great deal of empathy for the parents, who had tried a variety of medical and behavioral interventions to no avail.

Steve had agreed to meet me in the living room with his parents present. I was told that this was a major concession, which was linked to getting a pizza after the session was over. He was a very good-looking, blue-eyed, blond, and fair-complexioned adolescent of slight build and intense demeanor. I intuitively took a distant seat from him. After being introduced, I sat in silence for a few moments, intermittently making eye contact with Steve and allowing my gaze to wander freely about the room.

"What are *you* looking at, *asshole!*" was his opening comment to me.

Steve's mother winced and his father gave him a round of reprimands and warnings that he shrugged off absently while he monitored me with sidelong glances. I assured Steve's parents that this was a unique form of greeting and insisted that no apology was required. I commented on Steve's "Cannibal Corpse" T-shirt and asked if he knew enough about heavy metal groups to give me the name of a hot CD I could get for my nephew's birthday.

"I know a *lot* about heavy metal!" he snapped. He struggled out of his slouch into a semi-erect sitting position. He visually checked in with his parents, then asked warily, "Why did you come here?"

"To meet you," I replied. "What's *your* guess?"

Steve smiled cagily. "You came here to help me with my *space issue.*"

"And what's that about?"

"Well, you know, about how I don't like to go out of my room, and don't like it when people get too close to me."

"Well, that's interesting. Am I too close right now? I'll consider moving if you can show me a better place to sit."

Steve's parents exchanged uncomfortable glances. I asked Steve if we could visit alone for a while, and his parents left. Changing the subject, I told him that I had seen some of the rock group logos he had drawn at school and asked if he was keeping them in a file or book. He looked directly at me, murmuring that he didn't have a book, and I suggested that we meet in my office and put a book together for his logos and pictures of "hot bands."

"You'll get me a book for my logos?" he asked.

"I'm finding it hard to hear you, Steve. Why don't you point to a chair that's closer but not too close. I'll sit down and you check out the distance. Then we'll be able to talk better."

He pointed to a chair that was closer and I sat down. When I asked him if he was comfortable he said he wasn't, so I asked him to point out another chair. We went back and forth for a while. I could see that his breathing had become shallow, and he began to wring his hands as he struggled to figure out how close or far away I should be.

"Steve, I get the feeling that you need some breathing room now," I said in a neutral tone. "I think I'll just go outside for awhile."

"What about the logos?" he asked quickly.

"I'll make you a deal," I said. "I'll work things out with your teacher and parents for the logo book, if you'll do a role play with me and talk about what happens inside you when you get angry."

Steve frowned, pursed his lips, and stared at the floor as his breath accelerated. "I *hate* role play!" he said, clenching his fists.

"I get the point, Steve—no role play," I said, sensing that he was close to throwing something at me. "But, according to your teacher, you're a very smart guy. Can you tell me what you're feeling in your body—right now?"

"No—and I think that's a stupid question!"

"All right, let's try another one. Did you think I was telling you what to do a moment ago?"

"I don't like it when people tell me what to do! I like to do my own thing. I'm not an adult but I have civil rights. It's a free country. And I can sit in my room if I want to."

"You're absolutely right, Steve, you can sit in your room and be free. But I wonder how much you actually get to do in your room. By the way, are you interested in girls?"

"Definitely."

"Then how do you get to meet girls if you sit in your room all the time? I'm ready to help you learn how to meet and talk to girls—but only if you're interested."

Steve's face flushed and his countenance brightened. He stood up and dug his fingernails into his palms, making fists, then releasing them. "You'd really help me with talking to girls?"

"That's right," I said. "All you have to do is come to my office."

Steve clenched his fists. "No office," he said abruptly.

I stood up, smiled, and said, "I get the point, Steve."

Steve returned my smile and breathed more deeply. I told him I thought this was a good time to call it a day. He expressed his relief at my departure. Assuring his parents that things had gone well, I made an appointment for the following week.

I saw Steve at his home for three more sessions, after which he consented to come to my office. I had decided to use an approach based on the **Rosenberg Integrative Body Psychotherapy (IBP)** model of **character style**, using observable breath and body cues as indicators of internal processes. In IBP terms, Steve's personality had been shaped by a **high inundation** sensitivity: he was quick to feel inundated or invaded by what is usually regarded as routine interpersonal contact. This experience appeared to be triggered by both physical proximity and verbal communication. Steve was not receptive to offers of friendly contact, and he could be explosively reactive when he perceived that suggestions, hints, requests, and even factual information were a way of someone trying to control him. His basic interpersonal stance in life was: *Nobody can tell me what to do.* This is why attempts to shape and manipulate his behavior had not been successful.

When working with this aspect of Steve's character style it was important to understand that his oppositional behavior had two "flavors" that could be related to infantile and adolescent developmental stages. Observing the hair-trigger reactivity of Steve's behavior, there seemed to be a terrible two's (**separation-individuation**) quality about how he related to his parents and teachers. At other times there was an adolescent flavor, as expressed by his declarations of freedom and other assertions of his legal rights. He was both stubborn as a toddler and explosive as a rebellious teenager. Thus it was important not to get into power struggles with him. Wielding authority ultimately led to emotional close-downs and escalated behavior. At the same time it was also important not to walk on eggshells around him out of fear. For most of his life, Steve had created a sense of autonomy and regulated his outer environment by shutting everyone out and attacking them. His inner world was a closed system, highly resistant to the input of others. His basic attitude of *nobody can tell me what to do* gave him the breathing room he required to regulate what came in and out of his circle of experience, but it also isolated him and impoverished his quality of life. This is why he wanted people *not too close, but not too far away.* (For a brief summary of the IBP theory of character style, see Appendix 3.)

I worked in sessions with Steve's automatic no, helping him feel in control so that he didn't feel vulnerable to being inundated. I stated frankly that it was entirely his business if he wanted to spend his life only being able to relate to people by being aggressive or pushing them away—that I had no intention of forcing him to leave the closed world of his bedroom. On the other hand, if he wanted to get certain things that were important to him, I would be glad to help.

When Steve realized that I did not have an agenda to change him or make him feel bad about his behavior, he began to feel more at ease with me. He surprised me by his willingness to do breathing exercises, which helped him "move through" the rigid, reactive tendencies of his character style that led him to oppose indiscriminately whatever came toward him. The process was arduous, repetitive, and moved forward in small steps, as indicated in the following dialogue from one of our sessions.

"Steve, what would it be like if you joined your family at the dinner table tonight?"

"No way!"

"I notice that your leg is very busy. If it had a voice, what do you think it would say?"

"That's a very stupid question—but I do know the answer. It would say: 'I feel like kicking somebody'!"

"Why do you think it wants to kick somebody?"

"Why do you keep asking me tricky questions?"

"Well, I know that freedom is important to you, and I'm wondering if you'd like to be free of having to kick someone every time you feel angry. I know a breathing exercise that could help. But it might be too hard for you."

"I can do it—I'll show you!"

I taught Steve how to breathe *into* and *through* a "bad thought," which intrigued him. (Steve didn't like to talk about feelings because he couldn't identify them, so we referred to thoughts instead.) Alternate nasal breathing had novelty value for Steve, and he was eager to demonstrate his new skill to his parents and teacher. After several months Steve was able to independently practice relaxation techniques that lowered his reactivity threshold and made it easier to take in messages, information, and contactful overtures from those who cared about him. During one session that seemed to be going well, we had the following exchange:

> "Steve, now that you seem to be feeling nice and relaxed, I'm going to ask you another question. Try and be aware of what's going on in your body as you listen. Now here's the question: How would you feel about sitting five steps closer to your classroom door tomorrow?"
>
> "No!"
>
> "What are you thinking right now?"
>
> "That these questions really piss me off!"
>
> "Steve, when I *ask* you something, does it sound like you're being *told* what to do?"
>
> "It's confusing."
>
> "What do you think?"
>
> "I think I get upset when people ask me to do things I don't want to do."

I suggested to Steve that he got upset because of *how he heard* things that were said to him. I defined it as a hearing and translation problem. My idea was to help him actually hear differently and to translate what was being said in a way that didn't "piss him off" so much. We had a lot of fun comparing *asking* statements to *commands* by talking about what would happen if General Patton met Sergeant Bilko. I joked with Steve about needing a "translation time" instead of a "calm time" when he got upset. When Steve reacted negatively to a request, I often told him he needed to put in his "hearing aid."

Playfulness and humor go a long way in helping client and therapist feel lighter and more hopeful about issues of character style.

As my work with Steve progressed I formulated a set of intervention guidelines for Steve's parents and teachers. The guidelines were based on observations and insights from our work over a period of six months. Many of these suggestions have wider applications and can be incorporated into Positive and Multi-Element Program models.

INTERVENTION GUIDELINES FOR HIGH INUNDATION CHARACTER STYLE WITH A DEVELOPMENTALLY DISABLED CHILD OR ADOLESCENT

1. Maintain an approach of positive therapeutic indifference.

Take a step back and don't be highly invested in changing the behavior in question. Don't be a figure to fight against. You care, but you are not invasive with your concerns. Use phrases such as:

It's up to you.

I'm not here to tell you what to do—I'm here to love/teach you.

I would like to ask you a direct question. Are you ready to hear me?

I won't get into an argument with you over this. Think it over and we'll talk later.

When I give you information, please tell me when you've had enough.

I will be brief and direct so that you don't feel overwhelmed by me.

I respect you, and expect that you will respect me.

Positive therapeutic indifference does not mean being aloof or cool. Your intonation, phrasing, and demeanor reflect that you understand the experiential dilemma the young person is struggling with. You are making your best effort to cut him some slack without compromising yourself. You are not there to make him different, but to be of help when he is ready to ask.

2. Speak frankly. If you have been attacked or hurt by the disabled youngster, then, when the timing is right, explain how that made you feel. Explain that you are not holding a grudge, but may need to keep your distance for a specified period of time because your feelings were hurt.

Rogerian client-centered therapy, gestalt therapy, and IBP place great importance on *authenticity*. This is not so in some analytic and family systems approaches, and is rarely discussed in behavioral circles. In working with the disabled person, *modeling* is essential. You have to be real so that they can also be real. Conscious therapeutic disclosure has to be differentiated from countertransference reactions, which are unconscious and seep into the therapeutic relationship unchecked. By taking care of yourself, you are modeling an important lesson for the child. Withdrawal is not punitive when you explain yourself in the context of a positive, caring relationship. You are neither punishing nor abandoning the child. You are openly defining the parameters of the relationship and giving yourself a break so that you will not unconsciously abandon your own needs or close down emotionally in order to sustain a relationship under duress.

Steve's parents and teacher agreed to leave messages for me when there were incidents of aggression. If Steve had an aggression between sessions I told him I was on "red alert" about getting hit. I spoke openly about not wanting to be hit by him and stated that I would be on "yellow alert" until he had no more than one aggression per month. It was important for him to know that his dangerous behavior affected our relationship, and that, even though I believed he had no intentions of hitting me, I would have to play it safe until his aggressive behavior was eliminated.

3. Play a game called Doing the Opposite.

Steve refused to role play at first so we talked about situations in which someone else does the opposite of what might be expected. For example, Mr. Jones approaches Mr. Dixon with outstretched hand and says good morning. Mr. Dixon says goodbye and walks away. A teacher comes into the classroom, has a tantrum, and gets told to take a calm time by the students. Parents tell their child that they are no longer allowed to do chores or clean up their room.

Steve enjoyed this game immensely and in his enthusiasm ended up doing role plays even though he knew I had asked him to. But of course at that point it was *his* game and not mine.

4. Experiment with distance and boundaries in the natural context of your relationship.

As illustrated in the opening dialogue with Steve, always take a distant position and relinquish the control of regulating closeness. Once Steve felt he was in control, the give-and-take interplay of negotiation became possible. In working with Steve I was very careful to always set boundaries at the beginning of our meetings. It was a way of being respectful about his interpersonal problem. After a few sessions, both the time it took to do this as well as the distance between us shrank drastically.

5. Never argue. State your point and walk away whenever the conversation becomes heated.

As soon as an argumentative tone emerges on either side, there are systems in collision and there can be no meaningful exchange. At that point talking itself is the problem. It is better to have a brief but explicit understanding of disagreement, or, even better, a silent understanding of disagreement.

Steve did his best to draw me into disputes and arguments, assiduously seeking an arena of conflict, something to bump up against. I simply told him that I didn't like to argue and tried to help him become aware of the tone and inflection of his speech when he was becoming argumentative. At times I simply laughed or remained silent, and waited for him to approach me in a positive way.

I worked with Steve for eight months and followed up a year later. I was happy to hear that physical aggression was a thing of the past. Apparently he was still quite argumentative and very committed to having things his own way—but then so are many of us. It sounded as if the adults in Steve's life had come to a better understanding of how he felt and thought, and were giving him the space he needed not to feel inundated by the demands of life. I also got the feeling, based partly on our work together, that Steve was continuing to "breathe" his way through the intense sensations that tended to overwhelm him from within. It was my hope that his *automatic no* would come to be balanced by continued contact with caring people and a developing ability to trust and be concerned about others.

18

PERPETRATION:

The Pervasive Dilemma of Sexual Abuse

Although the numbers vary from study to study, there is evidence that up to 90 percent (Baladarian 1986) of developmentally disabled individuals are sexually abused at some time in their lives, and that one-third will have suffered abuse before the age of 18. There is a dangerous lack of awareness about the risk of abuse for this population. People somehow can't imagine that this is happening. It is also difficult to digest the fact that 97–99 percent of the perpetrators are known to and trusted by the victims (Baladarian 1991). I found it hard to believe, for example, that a 16-year-old severely autistic male who was referred to me had been molested by his male psychiatrist over a four-year period. I was quickly convinced, however, at our first meeting, when this young man stopped dead in his tracks at the door, screamed, slammed the door, and bolted. Although I attempted many different approaches, I was unable to establish a therapeutic alliance with him, and was ethically obliged to refer him to a female therapist. This was a sobering experience for me.

It is quite common for workers in this field to be oblivious to the impact of sexual abuse because there is often no immediately observable effect on the person they are working with. An autistic child with limited expressive speech cannot process the experience of abuse by talking about it, and may not exhibit obvious behavioral effects for some time. The crisis passes, everything seems to be all right, vigilance is relaxed, and again the disabled child is vulnerable to victimization. Hence the need for intensified education and dialogue with professionals and others involved in this field.

To illustrate this point I would like to relate the stories of two adolescents whose personal histories fit patterns that are all too common. Although the first is ostensibly the perpetrator and the second the victim, they were both victims of circumstances that were beyond their control. There are no simple solutions, but increased supervision and alertness to the causes and conditions of abuse can certainly reduce the frequency of its occurrence. In a climate of greater social awareness and a willingness to take quick preventive action, perhaps we can reduce the prevalence of traumatic injury and damaged lives.

Wayne was referred to me in a highly charged atmosphere of legal liability and alarm because he and a peer had been implicated in an attempted rape with a girl in the changing room at the school gym. Wayne was 18 years old, stocky, sporting a multicolored, close-cropped hairstyle and the requisite paraphernalia that accompany contemporary clothing for his age group. Behind this well-put-together veneer was a tired-looking youth with compressed features who squinted as he spoke. He was not at all pleased about the mandated counseling. He was sticking to his story that the girl who had "ratted him out" had propositioned him and his friend earlier in the day and suggested they meet after her swimming class. According to Wayne, she had promised that she would "do them both," so "why the hell was he in trouble?" He was surly and monosyllabic in his responses to my questions. He also seemed to be completely exhausted by everything in life, as if each breath was a monumental effort for him. I was no stranger to adolescent ennui, but Wayne struck me as someone who was only half alive, and just barely hanging on.

As I read Wayne's lengthy file between sessions it struck me that, after all he had suffered as a child, it was a miracle he was in fact alive and able to sustain any kind of human relationship at all. He was found at the age of 2 in a commercial garbage container with two broken arms and in a state of starvation. Throughout various foster home placements he had exhibited a need to eat almost continuously and would gorge himself until he became sick. When Wayne was 6, his foster father was caught in the middle of a photo shoot with two other adults committing lewd acts involving Wayne. Due to severe behavioral problems he had to be removed from his next three placements.

Unimpressed by the concept of mandated counseling, Wayne came to sessions sporadically at first, but when he showed up he did become increasingly willing to talk about painful experiences. At times he was able to recall fleeting images of being sexually abused. No feeling arose as he spoke to me about these events in his characteristic droning monotone. I was careful not to elicit the expression of any feeling he might not be able to contain.

At the age of 13, Wayne was in another foster home in which he was forced to have sex with both parents. It always started in the shower. His foster father would come into the shower and force him to have oral sex. Then he would take him to the master bedroom where he forced him to have sex with his foster mother. Wayne told me that he was very afraid of his foster father, who threatened to kill him if he ever said a word to anybody. He said that in the beginning he hated what was done to him, but later on got to "like it a bit." From beginning to end he always knew it was wrong, and he felt very bad about what he was doing even when he experienced a good deal of physical pleasure.

Wayne was heavily medicated by a psychopharmaceutical cocktail that gave me the impression of strategic bets laid in a game of roulette. This accounted in large part for his drowsiness and listless movements. I regularly gave him permission to be angry, and once he had determined that I was not there to judge and blame him he began coming to sessions with little prompting. I soon discovered that behind the drug-induced torpor was an angry, depressed, and extremely confused young man.

As with many youngsters who have been in the mental health system from an early age, Wayne had been the recipient of counseling services for the better part of his life. He had learned how to be a "good" client and could turn it on and off at will. At first I was surprised by his ability to talk about such painful experiences, but I later realized that he had been doing this for years. He was able to appear self-reflective and make the connections between current behavior and childhood abuse, expressing gratitude for having a "safe place" to talk. He also articulated a convincing intention to never again do to others what had been done to him. Because he would alternatively not show up for sessions, or pretend to fall asleep when he was in no mood to talk, he appeared to have integrated the principle of **intermittent reinforcement** from his own behavioral treatment, and was applying it to the therapists and care providers who worked with him. When Wayne had a good day, staff were ecstatic. When Wayne had a bad day, they seemed to suffer with him. He had learned that those who were currently responsible for his care were in some compassionate way attempting to compensate for his long ordeal of abuse. Part of Wayne's survival strategy was to "work" whatever system he found himself in, and I realized at the outset that I should not expect his relationship with me to be an exception.

Wayne's ability to con therapists, teachers, and care providers was both adaptive and maladaptive, as this allowed him to get short-term needs met but ultimately resulted in the loss of potential relationships. In short, there were different aspects of Wayne's personality that were not entirely out of his awareness, but which were so disconnected that his behavior was unpredictable and surprising even to himself.

This unpredictability manifested most strikingly three months prior to Wayne's departure. He had been coming to sessions regularly and had no serious problems in school or at his residence. He seemed perkier than usual, and even seemed to be coping well with a recent medication reduction. Then, to my dismay, I received a report alleging that Wayne had been involved in forced oral sex in the gym shower room with Bobby, a 16-year-old with Down's Syndrome.

In our first session after this allegation Wayne vacillated between belligerence and remorse. At the outset he denied he was involved, attempting to enlist me as an ally who might mitigate the consequences that were to follow. When that failed, he held his head in his hands and said he found it hard to admit because he was ashamed, embarrassed, and worried about what would happen to him. When I did not celebrate this admission to the extent he had hoped for, he looked at me and said, "Do you want to know what the real truth is?"

I nodded and said, "Yes, I do, and I want to believe you are able to tell me the truth."

Wayne paused, narrowed his eyes, and said, "I blacked out. I don't know what the hell happened."

I knew that this was quite possible, given the severity of his abuse and the general level of dissociation he lived with at the best of times, and yet I had the distinct feeling he was using "therapy talk" on the therapist. In that moment I wondered whether we could ever develop a relationship of mutual trust and openness. We had been thrust into each other's lives with a forced agenda and, given Wayne's long history of betrayal and abuse, there was no rational basis other than hope for expecting him to be truthful at that moment. What was relevant was that Wayne's sexual perpetration had happened in the shower, just as it had happened to him in the shower five years earlier. Whether he was telling the truth now about how it had happened was beside the point. The degree to which this was a volitional act as opposed to the eruption and acting out of a **state-bound experience** was relevant, but what was most important was the fact that someone with Wayne's history had been left unsupervised in the gym shower room.

I was eventually able to talk with Wayne about antecedent events leading up to this destructive encounter and, as he was insightful, I believe he was able to understand the importance of arousal cues and environmental cues in relation to his risk level for perpetration. He wrote a letter of apology to Bobby, but was very uneasy about discussing the impact of this experience on Bobby's life.

Prior to this event, Bobby, the Down's Syndrome victim, had been a mischievous and extremely affectionate child whose interests and way of relating were more like those of a 6-year-old than a 16-year-old. His degree of retardation was in the Moderate range, and he had severe expressive speech deficits. Bobby's teacher was surprised that he was able to actually convey what had happened to him, and for this reason was strongly convinced that a forced sexual act had occurred.

Further evidence that something of a traumatic nature had occurred was the emergence of AWOL and tantrum behavior soon after the incident. Bobby became surly, argumentative, and extremely demanding. He had always demonstrated attention-seeking behavior, but now he seemed to be angry and bitter, having lost his cheerful disposition. His behavior was very soon out of control, and staff at his group home were at a complete loss. Bobby refused to go to counseling appointments and would not engage in play therapy at his residence. He soon became isolative, ever more combative with peers, and nonresponsive to all therapeutic attempts to help him. For the first time in his life he was given medication trials, none of which was effective.

I was not directly involved in Bobby's case, but I did confer with his case manager and teacher, and I was able to observe his mood and behavior in educational and residential settings. It seemed that he was extremely depressed and unable to process the trauma of being sexually abused. His parents became so alarmed by his rapid deterioration that they brought him home and enrolled him in another school district. When I followed up a year later with Bobby's parents, they told me that he was doing better but that "he became a different person after that incident." They also implied that he had never regained his trusting, innocent charm.

Both Bobby and Wayne are links in a chain of perpetration that is sustained by a woeful lack of social awareness and vigilance. Given the high probability of sexual abuse happening in this population, it is imperative that caregivers and families be highly vigilant in family, educational, and other residential settings. We do not offer a clinical solution because there is no easy answer. Often what is needed is increased long-term supportive therapy, more carefully thought out risk management strategies, and a quicker legal response. Children and adolescents with disabilities are even more vulnerable than other children, and when they are sexually abused it is often very difficult to ascertain what happened and when.

Far too often, crimes against developmentally disabled victims go unprosecuted. Prosecutors are all too frequently reluctant to go to court when the principal witness is developmentally disabled, as their testimony may not be weighted strongly enough to carry the case. We

feel that stronger advocacy and legal follow-through for this population are essential if there is to be a reduction in the prevalence of abuse
generally, particularly in cases of repetitive predation.

At the 1994 annual meeting of the National Association of the
Dually Diagnosed, Dr. Nancy Birnbaum, who has been doing group
therapy with perpetrators for over 15 years, went on record to state
that it takes seven years for therapy with sexual perpetrators without
disabilities to have a significant effect. What to say then about the
length of therapy for the disabled? When therapists sit in their offices
with the growing numbers of children who have personal histories
similar to Wayne's, what can they hope to achieve? And is society ready
to foot the bill for therapeutic attempts whose outcome is uncertain?
On the other hand, if therapeutic services are not provided, what will
be the consequences for the abused individuals and for society at
large?

A few years ago, the political agenda was to remove children from
the home at the first hint of abuse. Currently family reunification is a
priority. But regardless of shifting political winds, workers in this field
are hamstrung by absurdly large caseloads as well as limited time and
options. Placement decisions are often made in crisis with poor
assessment parameters and delayed follow-up. Politicians, professionals, and families who are involved with the developmentally disabled
population need to feel a greater sense of urgency about these issues
and take affirmative action—now!

My former client Wayne and I shared a very authentic moment
before he graduated. It was our last session and he was talking about
his preparations for leaving his group home and moving out on his
own. I asked him how he imagined he would deal with sexual arousal
when he found himself alone with someone weaker than he was. He
smiled and pulled out of his pocket a laminated list of *staying safe*
reminders we had worked on. Then a cloud of emotion seemed to
come over him and he said somberly, "I just hope that I don't lose it.
Not this list, you know—I just hope that I don't go blank like I
do—and really *lose it*."

19

COMPASSION'S SHADOW:

The Dangers of Countertransference

I am standing in line at the grocery store. Nearby, I see a young, nonverbal autistic adolescent with whom I have been working. She takes a couple of steps and then starts to flap her arms. She repeats this process a few times.

Next, she looks around. She drops her arms and begins walking normally. I call out, "Hey, Diane."

She looks up at me and smiles. She says, "Hey, how are you doing?" Then she gasps. "Oh, you caught me. Gosh, it gets exhausting pretending to be autistic. Don't tell anyone, okay?"

During my first few years working with the developmentally disabled, I had dreams of this kind about two different autistic clients. Later, in talking with colleagues, I found that it is common for those working intensively with autistic individuals to have such dreams. These dreams are typically about lower-functioning clients with autism about whom the dreamer has grown to care deeply.

When working with children, it is natural to develop nurturing, protective, or affectionate feelings. Such feelings may be even more pronounced when faced with the isolation, limitations, and sadness of many children with Pervasive Developmental Disorders or dual diagnoses. Though the literature on **countertransference** with children is quite limited (Marshall 1979), a common theme in the existing literature is that therapists tend to recapitulate patterns from the parent–child relationship.

Feelings of grief or disappointment can be particularly difficult to face for either parents or professionals. Some who specialize in work with families of the developmentally disabled have noted that family members face an initial shock when learning about their child's disability. Many will then experience new feelings of sorrow, grief, or disappointment at major stages of their child's development when they reflect on opportunities and experiences that the developmentally disabled child will not have access to. As therapists and other professionals develop protective, nurturing, parental feelings for a disabled child, similar feelings of grief, disappointment, or sorrow may emerge about who the child might have been and the limitations that his disability does have on his life.

Americans do not generally like to face limitations or loss, and denial is one common way of dealing with feelings of grief. Regarding the developmentally disabled, there has been a strong, positive movement in America toward normalization. This movement emphasizes giving these children the same opportunities and experiences that nondisabled children have. For families and professionals to work together toward this goal of increased access is extremely important. It is also important, though, that one's efforts in this direction not cause an inability or unwillingness to honestly face the limitations that disabilities bring to children's lives—particularly for lower-functioning clients. Such denial is unhealthy for a family and is particularly dangerous for the therapist.

There is a good deal of literature (Devereux Foundation n.d., Mogenson 1992, Wilker et al. 1981) about the psychological importance of being able to work through complex feelings of grief, loss, or sorrow. From Freud's (1917) time on, this process of "working through" has been referred to as mourning. Working through these kinds of emotions is essential to psychological development and genuine, complete interpersonal relationships. Failure to mourn losses can lead to feelings of hollowness, emptiness, depression, or anxiety.

If a therapist cannot honestly face complex feelings of this kind when they arise in relation to a client, this may lead to a superficial quality in the therapeutic relationship. It may also give the client the unfortunate impression that this relationship is not a good place to bring such feelings. Furthermore, denying such feelings over time may ultimately lead to poor clinical judgment and difficulty developing effective treatment plans.

I saw an extreme example of this involving a colleague who had been working with the developmentally disabled for nearly fifteen years. Between 1990 and 1993, she went through a battle with breast cancer and the loss of both of her parents. During this period, *facilitated communication* was becoming increasingly popular for use with autistic clients with severe expressive speech impairments. In this method, a *facilitator* (a nondisabled family member or professional) would hold the autistic person's hand while he typed out answers to questions. The use of such communication boards was not new, but having someone actually holding the hand of the disabled person while he typed was quite controversial, as it was unclear whether the messages were coming from the autistic person or the facilitator. A significant number of families and professionals in the field were claiming that this method had brought about remarkable improvements in both children and adults. Some claimed that this method revealed that autistic people were actually not disabled in their cognitive, emotional, and interpersonal development but were simply unable to express themselves normally, so that the use of facilitated communication set them free to express who they were. On the other hand, a growing number of controlled studies were indicating that facilitators were clearly influencing the content of the messages typed.

This colleague was initially quite cautious about claims regarding facilitated communication, as was I. In 1993, she began experimenting with its use. Over the next few months, she became increasingly convinced that what her clients typed as she held their hands was coming solely from them. After she had been using this method for eight months, she revealed to me that she had become convinced that autistic people were clairvoyant, claiming that the content of their facilitated communications clearly indicated that they knew things that they could not have known by means other than clairvoyance. I remember explaining to her that an increasing number of studies were coming out that indicated that the communications generated in this way could not reliably be ascribed to the client whose hand was being held, and that it appeared that the facilitators were consistently, albeit unconsciously, affecting the content of the communications. She showed me how there were actually a few thousand people around the country who shared her belief that not only were facilitated communications valid, but that they actually proved that autistics were developmentally normal and had clairvoyant capacities.

Despite the claims of university researchers, my colleague and a number of other experienced professionals adamantly claimed that they were certain that they were not influencing the communications. For me, meeting with this colleague and a number of others became a valuable experience in understanding the meaning of doing something *unconsciously*. Each of these people with whom I spoke said, quite reasonably, that they would know if they were or weren't moving another person's hand. I was reminded that Jung had once said, "for the unconscious is really unconscious" (Ribi 1990, p. 115). When one acts on an unconscious motivation, one really doesn't know one is doing so. Even for professionals in the field of psychology, accepting that we ourselves may be acting out unconscious fantasies can be very difficult to see and understand.

One day, as I was speaking with this colleague, it struck me that it was as if she had gotten lost in one of those dreams discussed above. Trying to deal with her illness, the loss of her parents, and facing feelings of grief and loss at work was more than she could bear, so, invoking a denial of unbearable aspects of reality, she became increasingly caught up in fantasy. Finally, when she began believing that the clairvoyant capacities of people with autism were a reflection of the fact that they were angelic incarnations, she realized that she had gone too far and had to change her field of work and seek professional help.

Although the example of this colleague's experience is extreme, the unconscious use of denial as a defense against feelings of grief about clients' disabilities, particularly when those clients are children, is more common than is generally acknowledged. For those working in this field, it is important both personally and professionally to try to be aware of such feelings when they arise and to work through them consciously, seeking support or supervision when necessary.

Another difficult issue which comes up often for professionals working with the developmentally disabled is feeling powerless or helpless. Given the complexity and severity of some of these children's problems, the difficulties involved in helping them, and the limited available resources, such feelings are natural.

Throughout this book, we present numerous interventions that have been effective with developmentally disabled clients with whom we have worked. However, it is important to acknowledge that, on a day-to-day level, it is often difficult to see changes, and it can be extremely frustrating to see someone improve and then regress. These kinds of experiences can come up in therapy with clients of any kind, but progress is usually slower with mentally retarded or developmentally disabled clients than it is with their nondisabled peers, and improvements are often highly dependent on a stable and supportive external environment.

Given these facts, occasional feelings of inadequacy and frustration are normal. Again, facing them honestly is important. We have also found that working cooperatively with other professionals is important in mitigating the negative effects of such feelings. For clients with multiple problems, a team approach to treatment involving parents and teachers as well as speech therapists, behavioral experts, psychotherapists, physicians, occupational therapists, and psychiatrists when appropriate is most likely to provide the support that is needed.

Unfortunately, when feelings of inadequacy are not faced consciously, one result often seems to be that different people in a child's life will blame each other for difficulties in treatment. Not wanting to face the fact that it is difficult to help some people and that one's own ability as a professional is limited, one professional may be tempted to blame another for a child's regression or lack of progress. A behavioral expert may blame a teacher for not implementing his plan, a teacher may blame a psychiatrist for not prescribing medications that make a child more capable of learning, and so on. Again, when various people involved in a child's treatment find themselves blaming one another, it may be useful to reflect on whether feelings of helplessness underlie these problems and whether a meeting to take a more collaborative approach may be helpful. For children with complex problems, it is extremely rare that any one approach in isolation will be effective in the long run; a collaborative approach involving a multi-element plan is most likely to be genuinely helpful.

Another issue related to feelings of hopelessness or inadequacy that bears mentioning is the tendency to deny these feelings by imagining oneself to be more powerful or effective than one actually is. Families of the developmentally disabled naturally would very much like to see their children cured, and so it is quite tempting for professionals to assert—either openly or subtly—that they do or may have a cure for these children. It is very important for professionals to be wary of this temptation and for families to be wary of professionals making such claims.

Some professionals try to bolster their sense of efficacy by practicing in areas outside of their expertise. It is not uncommon in working with the developmentally disabled to see direct care professionals trying to do psychotherapy, behavioral experts suggesting vitamin therapies, psychotherapists trying to do speech therapy, or psychiatrists trying to design behavioral interventions. Clearly, it is useful to have an awareness of treatment methods outside of one's primary area of expertise, and pursuing additional training can be a positive effect of feeling that one's current knowledge is inadequate to some of the challenges that one faces. However, it is important to be honest with oneself and others about the scope of one's professional practice and the likely positive effects of any given treatment. *In the treatment of the dually diagnosed and developmentally disabled, amelioration of specific symptoms, increased independence and improved quality of life are generally realistic treatment goals, while a cure generally is not.*

The final issue that we would like to raise regarding countertransference is establishing and maintaining appropriate **boundaries**. It is often a standard practice for teachers, therapists, and other professionals working with the developmentally disabled *not* to maintain the same kinds of boundaries as they would with nondisabled clients, and in many cases this is a necessity. For example, most therapists and teachers working with adolescents avoid physical touch. However, when working with lower-functioning, developmentally disabled clients with limited verbal skills, regardless of their age, it is sometimes impossible to communicate effectively or develop rapport without a considerable degree of physical contact.

The specific nature of one's role as well as the needs and developmental level of the clients or students with whom one is working will be determining factors in what kinds of boundaries one establishes. While flexibility in one's approach can be essential to success with this population, failure to maintain appropriate boundaries can lead to confusion for all involved, to poor modeling of boundaries for the clients, and to complex interpersonal problems. While we support flexibility in boundary setting with certain individuals, we feel that professionals should always ask themselves *why* they are making an exception in any given case and should discuss these issues with colleagues when in doubt.

Some of the issues that confound the establishing of appropriate boundaries and the problems that can arise when these are not established and maintained in a clear way are illustrated by a case involving a colleague named William.

William was an experienced social worker who had worked in hospital settings as well as in private practice with children and adults (though not with the developmentally disabled) when he was hired to serve as a clinical case manager for three children's group homes. The clients in these group homes were all developmentally disabled boys. Most of them had been severely abused and neglected. Part of William's job was to work with the Department of Children's Services and the Department of Mental Health, who provided funding for these boys' placements, in helping to develop current behavioral treatment plans and determine plans for their future. He was also expected to provide individual and group psychotherapy as needed. Initially, William was quite effective in providing case management and individual therapy to clients who were going through a difficult time. However, he found group therapy challenging because of the group dynamics and the high degree of behavioral acting out. He also struggled with designing behavioral plans, as he had not received professional training in this area.

After William had been at this job for three months, Thanksgiving was two weeks away. William asked the supervisors of each of the group homes what the kids would be doing for the holiday. At two of the group homes, residential staff were planning on taking kids to their homes for Thanksgiving dinner. At the third home, though, the supervisor reported that the kids would be remaining at the group home to eat a meal donated by a local restaurant. William felt that this was a sad situation and that the residents deserved a semblance of a normal childhood. So he and his fiancée decided to pick some of the children on Thanksgiving day for a meal at their home.

William's motivation was sincere, and the Thanksgiving dinner went well. However, over the course of the subsequent two weeks, he began having doubts about the wisdom of inviting his clients to his home. A client named Jack began perseverating in therapy sessions on sexual fantasies about William's fiancée. Another client named Freddy insisted that William and his fiancée adopt him. Later in the week, when Freddy got into an argument with one of his peers, he ran away from the group home and showed up four hours later on William's front steps.

Freddy ran away to William's home a number of times over the following months. Six months later, when William had to tell Freddy that his social worker had decided to move him to another group home, Freddy took it very personally. He said, "Man, it's because I came over to your house, isn't it? That's why you're kicking me out!" He then attacked William with a chair, which led to a physical restraint.

In Central Asia, there is a traditional metaphor that says that compassion and wisdom are like the two wings of an eagle; it needs both to fly to its destination. Similarly, in order to work effectively with the developmentally disabled, we must combine our sincere and positive compassionate responses with wisdom based on training and study, discussion with colleagues, and past experience.

It is also very important to question our own assumptions about our work. Though a compassionate, caring approach is essential in this field, we must also look in the shadows of our compassion for unconscious countertransference reactions such as grief, hopelessness, or overinvolvement.

APPENDICES

APPENDIX 1
Boundary Basics

1. A boundary is an energetic, self-generated demarcation of one's self from others. It's where *I* end and *you* begin. Boundaries provide the basis of contact with others, regulating what comes into our circle of experience, and what we keep out of our circle of experience.
2. A person needs a boundary to have a sense of self. Unboundaried individuals often have an internal feeling or create an external impression of either being "not there" or "all over the place."
3. A person with weak boundaries is susceptible to being overwhelmed by stimulatory input, which can lead to mental and emotional fragmentation. People with disabilities are often helpless and vulnerable to abuse in states like this.
4. When a person has rigid boundaries, interpersonal contact is reduced, which can lead to isolation and a diminished sense of well-being.
5. The greater our ability to be aware of bodily cues and changes in breathing, the easier it is to know what our boundary patterns are and how they affect our relationships. Thus an important objective for families, teachers, and clinicians is to learn to read these cues and teach our children.

APPENDIX 2
Covert Reinforcement

Covert reinforcement is an approach that grew out of standard differential reinforcement procedures. In standard reinforcement procedures, an external or *overt* reinforcer is given upon the occurrence of a desired behavior. In covert reinforcement, the process takes place in the *imagination* of the person who is trying to change.

In covert reinforcement, one imagines oneself engaging in a specific desired behavior and one then imagines oneself in a reinforcing scene. There are many studies that have empirically demonstrated that covert conditioning is effective in bringing about lasting behavioral changes for a wide range of presenting problems in adults (Cautela and Kearney 1984, Cautela and Wall 1980, Scott and Rosentiel 1975). The research that has been done on the use of this procedure with children (Cautela 1982, Groden and Cautela 1984, LaVigna and Donnellan 1986, Scott and Rosentiel 1975, Workman and Dickinson 1979a) has also shown encouraging results. In our own clinical experience, the use of modified forms of covert reinforcement has been very effective in helping children with disabilities to decrease a wide range of challenging behaviors.

Covert reinforcement also has a number of significant practical advantages, including that it is enjoyable and is easier and less expensive to implement than standard reinforcement schedules. Once a covert reinforcement sequence has been developed, a caregiver or therapist will ordinarily sit down with the child for between ten and fifteen minutes per day, during a quiet time, to practice the sequence. (Higher functioning clients can practice on their own once they have become familiar with the sequence.) We have also found that this procedure has a number of positive side effects, including its encouraging positive rapport between caregivers and children, desensitizing students to difficult situations (antecedents), encouraging normalization, and teaching relaxation exercises that have proven useful to clients in a variety of situations.

A simple form of covert reinforcement that has been used in a number of the studies on covert conditioning with children (Groden and Cautela 1984, Workman and Dickinson 1979a,b) is called *covert positive reinforcement* (CPR). In brief, CPR involves teaching clients to imagine themselves in a situation that has sometimes been an antecedent to a negative behavior. They then imagine performing a new target behavior and then immediately imagine a pleasant, reinforcing scene. This procedure is summarized as follows:

Simple Covert Positive Reinforcement (CPR)
Antecedent—New Response—Reinforcing Scene

In our work with developmentally disabled children, we have found that the use of CPR was most effective when combined in covert or imagined practice with other complementary techniques including thought stopping and relaxation. Therefore, the self-control triad (SCT) was used. "The SCT combines thought stopping, relaxation training, and CPR" (Cautela and Kearney 1984). This procedure is summarized as follows:

CPR paired with Thought Stopping and Relaxation
Antecedent—Stop—Relaxation—New Response—Reinforcing Scene

We have used this procedure successfully with a number of higher functioning, developmentally disabled clients. An example of this appears in Chapter 11.

With lower-functioning developmentally disabled clients, we have learned to use a modified form of the above, which we have found to be very effective. An example of the use of a modified form as described below appears in Chapter 1. With these clients, we still use CPR paired with thought stopping and relaxation, but we make a few significant modifications.

The first of these modifications is that rather than simply helping the child to imagine the sequence by verbally leading him through it as we would with a higher functioning or nondisabled client, we create a series of *pictures* with which to lead him through the process. These pictures may be photos of him doing the things he will imagine or drawings. We ordinarily mount each picture on an index card, writing a script on the back for the person who will be helping him. Using a script of this kind is important because if caregivers change the words used too much this can lead to confusion or mixed messages for the client. The pictures and script help the child *learn to imagine* the sequence. Once he has become familiar with the sequence, the use of the pictures is faded.

A second modification that we have had to make with some of our clients is to have the reinforcing scene be related to the situation in which the new behavior is occurring. For higher-functioning clients, it can sometimes be very useful to imagine a powerfully reinforcing scene that is unrelated to the behavior, for example, sitting on a beach in Hawaii. For lower-functioning clients this is sometimes confusing. With these clients, we may have the reinforcer be imagining receiving praise, attention, or tangible reinforcers in their natural environment.

The final modification that we have sometimes made is, once the child has become familiar with the sequence, if his new imagined response is not easily generalizing to real-life situations then we may engage the child in role plays of the sequence. These role plays can occur during a structured learning time as the covert reinforcement procedure does and/or in the midst of his daily schedule.

APPENDIX 3
The Rosenberg IBP Approach to Character Style

The IBP approach to character style working with developmental injuries is similar to that articulated by Dr. Stephen Johnson, whose book *Character Styles* (1994) successfully integrates *DSM* diagnosis, developmental theory, current schools of analytic thought, and practical interventions for everyday psychotherapy. The IBP energetic model incorporates a great deal of analytic and developmental theory as well but, as an active body- and breath-based therapy, the IBP way of talking about character style is in simpler, more experiential language. From the IBP perspective the primary environmental deficits or injuries to the self are related to *abandonment* and *inundation*. Individuals with the *Abandonment–Inundation* character style are more highly represented in the general population than the extremes of *High Abandonment* and *High Inundation* character style. The individual's character style is a response to the environmental deficit or sense of injury to self. Within the *abandonment–inundation* spectrum there are individuals whose areas of interpersonal conflict will be triggered more often by one than the other. An abused person may have been abandoned, but his characterological development and interpersonal style may have developed around protecting himself from inundation. Conversely, another abandoned and abused person may have experienced the abandonment as primary, and developed a protective character style along the lines of defending against abandonment. In Steve's case (see Chapter 17), we were working with the defensive behaviors related to *inundation*.

This is an overly simplified presentation of the IBP characterological approach; a more detailed explanation can be found in *The Intimate Couple* (Rosenberg and Kitaen-Morse 1996) and *Body, Self, and Soul* (Rosenberg et al. 1985).

Glossary

Anal stage: One of the stages of psychosexual development originally outlined by Freud. This stage usually occurs between ages 1 and 3 years. As the child faces toilet training, issues of autonomy and sensual gratification versus parental control and shame often arise. Freud postulated that how a child moves through this phase has a significant impact on subsequent development, particularly affecting issues such as self-control, cleanliness, flexibility, generosity, and creativity.

Antecedent: From behavioral psychology, the conditions immediately preceding the occurrence of a behavior. Understanding the antecedents to a particular behavior can often be useful in determining the function that the behavior serves. Also, particularly in positive programming, modifying antecedent conditions is recognized as one way of increasing or decreasing targeted behaviors.

Attention-deficit Hyperactivity Disorder (ADHD): Defined according to the *DSM-IV* as a disorder of childhood, with onset prior to age 7, involving significant difficulty in paying attention to tasks or conversations and involving impulsivity and/or hyperactivity.

Autism: A syndrome or disorder first described by Leo Kanner in 1943. Currently, autism is a diagnostic category in the *DSM-IV* and is defined as a pervasive developmental disorder with onset prior to age 3 involving significant impairment in social interactions, impairment in communication, and "restricted, repetitive and stereotyped patterns of behavior, interests and activities" (*DSM-IV* 1994).

Autistic encapsulation/autistic shell: A set of auto-generated (self-stimulatory) sensations that an autistic person uses to block out other input, which may be confusing, overwhelming, or terrifying.

Boundaries: Ways of separating aspects of oneself from aspects of another, or of demarcating within oneself discrete areas of intrapsychic functioning. Boundary work has become common to all forms of psychotherapy, but is most explicitly addressed in Gestalt Therapy and Rosenberg Integrative Psychotherapy. In Gestalt theory, good boundaries are regarded as essential for reciprocally satisfying contact between two individuals. In the Rosenberg model, boundaries are regarded as an energetic phenomenon, and boundary work has a broader and deeper application to intrapersonal and interpersonal issues, often through experiential exercises.

Boundary (Structural Family Therapy): In structural family therapy boundaries define subsystems within a family structure, and are *rigid*, *diffuse*, or *clear*, referring to the degree of involvement between individuals within subsystems as well as subsystems within the larger family structure. Helping families create more functional and developmentally appropriate boundaries is an essential part of restructuring a family system.

Character education: The attempt to explicitly teach and foster the development of character in children. The well-known and successful Character Counts program developed by the Josephson Institute of Ethics focuses on Six Pillars of Character: trustworthiness, respect for others, responsibility, fairness, caring, and citizenship. In working with lower-functioning clients, it is sometimes necessary to create a shorter, simpler list of key components of character.

Character style: Refers to interpersonal patterns, behaviors, and ways of experiencing life based on childhood coping responses, which have become rigid or automatic, interfering with individual fulfillment and interpersonal satisfaction. Character styles may be differentiated from *personality disorders* in that there is less psychopathology implied. In the Rosenberg IBP model, character style is viewed as a pattern of defensiveness or reactivity originating from early experiences of inundation and/or abandonment, which have become a barrier to intimacy.

Countertransference: A psychological concept originated by Freud, originally referring to unconscious reactions on the part of a therapist to a patient, generally seen as destructive to the therapeutic process. Since that time, this term has come to refer more generally to all of the therapist's personal reactions to a patient, which can be either helpful or destructive to the therapeutic process depending on how the therapist deals with them.

Covert reinforcement: Similar to standard behavioral reinforcement procedures in that reinforcement is delivered upon the occurrence of a specific, desired response. However, in *covert* reinforcement, this entire procedure occurs in the *imagination* of the subject. The subject imagines a specific antecedent situation and then a desired response; next the subject imagines receiving a reinforcer or imagines herself in a reinforcing scene (see Appendix 2).

Diagnostic overshadowing: The tendency on the part of clinicians to so focus on a person's diagnosis related to their developmental disability that they overlook the presence of other psychological/ psychiatric conditions that might benefit from treatment.

Differential reinforcement: A term from applied behavior analysis that refers to procedures involving the delivery of reinforcers contingent upon the occurrence of operationally defined behaviors.

DRO: Means the differential reinforcement of behavior that is other than or different from a behavior that is targeted for change.

Discrete trial learning: An instructional method from applied behavioral analysis popular in the treatment of autism and other developmental disabilities. In brief, one trial involves gaining the client's attention, giving him an instruction, using whatever level of prompt necessary to gain a desired response, and then immediately delivering a reinforcer. Trials are generally repeated many times with the level of prompt given for success being gradually faded.

DSM-IV: The *Diagnostic and Statistical Manual of Mental Disorders*, published by the American Psychiatric Association; provides mental health professionals with a standard nomenclature of psychopathology in children and adults.

Dually diagnosed: Technically indicates that a person has two significant *DSM-IV* diagnoses. In this context, one of these diagnoses is generally related to a developmental disability (e. g., Mental Retardation, Autism, etc.) and the other is related to another significant condition requiring treatment, such as a psychotic disorder, mood disorder, or anxiety disorder.

Echolalia: A disorder of speech characterized by the involuntary repetition of words or phrases that someone else has spoken.

Empathy: Refers to the capacity to put one's current concerns aside and attune to the experiential state of another person. In therapeutic work the emphasis is on being "energetically present" with a degree of understanding that lets the other person feel heard or understood.
    Empathic reflection refers to the accuracy and the means by which this understanding is conveyed to the other person.

Functional analysis: A term from behavioral psychology referring to a process of recording the details of specific behavioral incidents along with their antecedents and consequences in order to subsequently analyze this data to develop a hypothesis regarding the function or purpose that the behavior serves for the person who is exhibiting it.

High Inundation: An IBP term referring to an individual's tendency to be hypersensitive to environmental stimuli, particulary in the realm of interpersonal relations, leading to a feeling of being overwhelmed.

Histrionic: Refers to a formal *DSM-IV* Personality Disorder or personality style that may be characterized as dramatic, flighty, attention seeking, gregarious, shallow, fickle, with a tendency to dissociate.

Identified patient: A term used most frequently (though not exclusively) in family therapy implying that one individual is carrying the symptom or problem of the larger family system.

Intermittent reinforcement: see **Reinforcement**

Mental retardation: An Axis II disorder in the *DSM-IV*, defined as having a full-scale IQ under 70 with related impairment in social, educational, and work performance. Onset must occur prior to age 18.

Milieu therapy: In hospital or group home settings, attempting to create an environment that will have a therapeutic or healing effect on the patients or clients living in that setting. Discussion groups, rules, activity choices, and group contingency contracts may be elements of such an approach.

Mirroring: Refers to a developmental need for recognition, attention, and an approving reflection of what is communicated. Self psychology addresses mirroring in relation to the development of idealized selfobjects, the early need for a mirroring selfobject, and the need for twinship selfobjects, which may manifest as a selfobject transference in psychotherapy.

Object relations: A branch of psychodynamic psychology that developed initially in England. Klein, Fairbairn, Winnicott, and other analysts in England based their approach on Freud's theories but emphasized how early relationships, particularly between the infant and mother, become internalized as self–other (or self–object) representations, which would then continue influencing interpersonal relations.

Perseverative: Uncontrollably repeating a word, phrase, gesture, or thought.

Pervasive developmental disorders: A set of disorders in the *DSM-IV*, all of which begin in early childhood. Autism is one of the disorders that falls under this heading. When a child has significant and severe symptoms characteristic of the specific disorders in the grouping but does not meet the criteria for being diagnosed with any one of them, then they may receive a diagnosis of Pervasive Developmental Disorder, Not Otherwise Specified.

Positive programming: An approach to changing behaviors based in applied behavior analysis that focuses on assessing the function(s) of these destructive or socially inappropriate behaviors and then systematically teaching new replacement behaviors. A significant difference between positive programming and other behavioral approaches is not using punishment to bring about behavioral change.

Positive reinforcement: See **Reinforcement**

Projective identification: A term from object relations psychology that refers to a process whereby a person projects an aspect of himself onto someone else and then attempts to control that aspect of himself by controlling the other person.

Protective shell: see **Autistic Encapsulation/Autistic Shell**

Psychic reality: From Jungian psychology, the understanding that although something may not exist physically, it can have a valid existence as a content of the mind. Jung (1961) particularly observed how similar themes appeared in psychotic delusions, dreams, fantasies, art, literature, and religion, thereby theorizing that these psychic contents were not meaningless but were "connected with the objective behavior of the human psyche" (p. 99).

Psychodynamic: Refers to therapies sharing the assumption that personality and behavior are the result of the interplay of forces within the individual, with a focus on the mechanisms of the unconscious. These therapies include psychoanalysis, ego analysis, object relations therapy, and self psychology therapy.

Refueling: Occurs during what Margaret Mahler (1968) describes as the separation-individuation phase of development. Particularly during the practicing subphase, the child begins moving away from the mother to explore the outside world. However, he frequently returns to the mother to maintain a sense of safety and well-being. This process of periodically returning to the mother is described as *emotional refueling.*

Reinforcement: A term from behavioral psychology that refers to the delivery of a desired event or item immediately contingent upon the occurrence of a desired behavior with the intent of increasing the likelihood of this behavior's occurrence in the future.

   Positive reinforcement refers to a reward that is given for the occurrence or performance of a desired behavior and that presumably creates the motivation leading to a higher probability of the behavior occurring in the future.

   Intermittent reinforcement refers to the delivery of a reinforcer at random intervals and with no contingency, so that there is no way to predict when it will be delivered. This is regarded as the most powerful type of reinforcement because there is a sustained expectation that it could be delivered at any time. Slot machines in Las Vegas provide this type of reinforcement to those who play them.

Replacement behaviors: Specific adaptive behaviors that one attempts to teach a person to use instead of less adaptive behaviors that they have previously relied upon.

Rosenberg Integrative Body Psychotherapy (IBP): A body-oriented system of depth psychotherapy drawing from a spectrum of theoretical perspectives including object relations, self psychology, Gestalt therapy, Reichian therapy, bioenergetics, and transpersonal psychotherapy. IBP addresses family of origin issues, agency (giving up the self in the service of others), and character style by way of experiential processes that integrate verbal and cognitive methods with a body orientation and breath work, while working with boundaries, energetic presence, adaptive mental health skills, and sexuality.

Self-injurious behaviors (SIB): Behaviors that threaten to produce immediate bodily harm to the person who is engaging in them, for example, head banging, biting self, cutting self, and so on.

Separation-individuation: A phase of psychosocial development as described by Margaret Mahler (1972) lasting roughly from ages 6 months to 24 months. Mahler describes three subphases: hatching, practicing, and rapprochement. During this phase, the child's developing motor abilities allow him to begin exploring the outer world. He begins venturing away from the mother and developing a sense of himself as separate from the mother. Confidence and delight in this new sense of self and access to the outer world fluctuates with intense need for the mother's love and attention as the sense of individuality gradually stabilizes.

Splitting: A term from object relations psychology that refers to a psychological process whereby a person "separates contradictory feelings, self-representations, or object-representations from one another" (Gabbard 1994, p. 44). The person does this because what is negative, bad, destructive, or hateful threatens to overwhelm or contaminate what they experience as good, helpful, or nurturing.

State-bound experience: A term derived from the field of state-dependent learning, memory, and behavior. This refers to an experience that is associated with a certain level of arousal and an interpretation of environmental cues. Traumatic experiences are typically state-bound and tend to be repeated in an individual's life.

Structural family therapy: A systems approach to therapy, first developed in the 1960s by Salvador Minuchin (1978), which is based on the assumption that, if you change the structure and family system dynamics, the symptoms of the family and individuals within the family will be relieved.

Subsystem: A structural family therapy term referring to components of a whole family system that are defined in relational terms or keep it functioning by performing various tasks, for example, parental subsystem, sibling subsystem.

Theory of mind: A phrase derived from cognitive research done over the last decade that indicates that people with autism may have significant deficits in their ability to understand that other people *have minds*, that is, experience motivations, feelings, and thoughts.

Transference: A concept originated by Freud referring to a patient's projections onto the therapist. Typically, the content of these projections derives from unresolved childhood issues which may be addressed by the therapist.

Twinship bond: A self psychology term that refers to a developmental need for a selfobject that creates a feeling of likeness or sameness. Initially Kohut (1971, 1977, 1984) regarded the need for a twinship selfobject as one of the stages in the development of the grandiose self, but later suggested it might be part of an ongoing lifetime developmental process.

References

Ayers, A. J. (1979). *Sensory Integration and the Child.* Los Angeles: Western Psychological Services.

Baladarian, N. J. (1986). *Survivor: Special Edition.* Los Angeles: Los Angeles Commission on Assaults Against Women.

——— (1991). Sexual abuse of people with developmental disabilities. *Sexuality and Disability* 2 (4):323–333.

——— (1992). *Interviewing Skills to Use with Abuse Victims who Have Developmental Disabilities.* Washington, DC: National Aging Resource Center on Elder Abuse.

Baron-Cohen, S. (1995). *Mindblindness: An Essay on Autism and Theory of Mind.* Cambridge, MA: MIT Press.

Benson, B. A. (1992). *Teaching Anger Management to Persons With Mental Retardation.* Worthington, OH: International Diagnostic Systems, Inc.

Bettelheim, B. (1967). *The Empty Fortress.* New York: Brunner/Mazel.

Bion, W. R. (1977). *Seven Servants: Four Works by Wilfred R. Bion.* New York: Jason Aronson.

Buirski, P., ed. (1994). *Comparing Schools of Analytic Therapy.* Northvale, NJ: Jason Aronson.

Campbell, J. (1972). *Myths to Live By.* New York: Bantam.

Cautela, J. R. (1982). Covert conditioning with children. *Journal of Behavior Therapy and Experimental Psychiatry* 13:209–214.

Cautela, J. R., and Kearney, A. J. (1984). Covert conditioning. In *Encyclopedia of Psychology, vol. 1*, ed. R. J. Corsini, pp. 305–306. New York: Wiley.

Cautela, J. R., and Wall, C. (1980). Covert conditioning in clinical practice. In *Handbook of Behavioral Interventions*, ed. M. Hersen and A. S. Bellack, pp. 152–185. New York: Wiley.

Christopher, W., and Christopher, B. (1989). *Mixed Blessings.* Nashville: Abingdon.

Devereux Foundation (n.d.). *Parenting an exceptional child.* Unpublished workshop handout.

Diagnostic and Statistical Manual of Mental Disorders (1994). 4th ed. Washington, DC: American Psychiatric Association.

Donnellan, A. M., LaVigna, G. W., Negri-Shoultz, N., and Fassbender, L. L. (1988). *Progress Without Punishment: Effective Approaches for Learners with Behavior Problems.* New York: Teachers College Press.

Edward, J., Ruskin, N., and Turrini, P. (1981). *Separation-Individuation.* New York: Gardner.

Erikson, E. H. (1959). Identity and the life cycle. *Psychological Issues*, Monograph 1. New York: International Universities Press.

Freud, S. (1917). Mourning and melancholia. *Standard Edition* 14:243–258.

——— (1969). *An Outline of Psycho-Analysis*, trans. J. Strachey. New York: Norton.

Gabbard, G. O. (1994). *Psychodynamic Psychiatry in Clinical Practice: The DSM-IV Edition.* Washington, DC: American Psychiatric Press.

Grandin, T. (1995). *Thinking in Pictures.* New York: Doubleday.

Grandin, T., and Scariano, M. M. (1986). *Emergence: Labeled Autistic.* Novato, CA: Arena Press.

Gray, C. (1995). Social stories unlimited: social stories, comic strip conversations, and related instructional techniques. In *1995 Na-*

tional Conference on Autism Proceedings, pp. 137–141. Silver Spring, MD: Autism Society of America.

Greenberg, J. R., and Mitchell, S. A. (1983). *Object Relations in Psychoanalytic Theory*. Cambridge, MA: Harvard University Press.

Groden, J., and Cautela, J. R. (1984). The use of imagery procedures to reduce aberrant behavior in students labeled "trainable retarded." *Psychological Reports* 54:595–605.

——— (1988). Procedures to increase social interaction among adolescents with autism: a multiple baseline analysis. *Journal of Behavior Therapy and Experimental Psychiatry* 19:87–93.

Groden, J., Cautela, J., Prince, S., and Berryman, J. (1994). The impact of stress and anxiety on individuals with autism and developmental disabilities. In *Behavioral Issues in Autism*, ed. E. Schopler and G. B. Mesibov, pp. 177–194. New York: Plenum.

Hamilton, N. G. (1988). *Self and Others: Object Relations Theory in Practice*. Northvale, NJ: Jason Aronson.

Hanks, G. (1995). Communication training: success through symbols. In *1995 National Conference on Autism Proceedings*, pp. 383–388. Silver Spring, MD: Autism Society of America.

Happe, F. (1995). *Autism: An Introduction to Psychological Theory*. Cambridge, MA: Harvard University Press.

Henry, D., Peterson-Vita, E., Piliero, C., et al. (1996). *Guidelines for Treatment of Sexually Disordered and Offending Adolescents*. Unpublished manuscript, Devereux Foundation.

Hillman, J. (1975). *Re-Visioning Psychology*. New York: Harper Collins.

Hobson, R. P. (1990). On psychoanalytic approaches to autism. *American Journal of Orthopsychiatry* 60:324–336.

Hoffman, L., ed. (1982). *The Evaluation and Care of Severely Disturbed Children and Their Families*. New York: SP Medical & Scientific Books.

Johnson, S. M. (1994). *Character Styles*. New York: Norton.

Jung, C. G. (1961). *Memories, Dreams, Reflections*. New York: Vintage.

Kadzin, A. E. (1973). Covert modeling and the reduction of avoidance behavior. *Journal of Abnormal Psychiatry* 81:87–95.

———— (1974). Covert modeling, model similarity, and reduction of avoidance behavior. *Behavior Therapy* 5:325–340.

———— (1975). Covert modeling, imagery assessment and assertive behavior. *Journal of Consulting and Clinical Psychology* 43:716–724.

Klein, M. (1948). *Contributions to Psycho-Analysis: 1921–1945*. London: Hogarth.

———— (1975). *Envy and Gratitude and Other Works: 1946–1963*. New York: Free Press.

Kohut, H. (1971). *The Analysis of the Self*. New York: International Universities Press.

———— (1977). *The Restoration of the Self*. Madison, CT: International University Press.

———— (1984). *How Does Analysis Cure?*, ed. A. Goldberg. Chicago: University of Chicago Press.

Kramer, S., and Akhtar, S. (1994). *Mahler and Kohut*. Northvale, NJ: Jason Aronson.

LaVigna, G. W., and Donnellan, A. M. (1986). *Alternatives to Punishment: Solving Behavior Problems with Non-Aversive Strategies*. New York: Irvington.

LaVigna, G. W., and Willis, T. J. (1997). Severe and challenging behavior: counter-intuitive strategies for crisis management within a nonaversive framework. *IABA Positive Practises* II(2):9–17.

Lignugaris-Kraft, B., McCuller, G. L., Exum, M., and Salzberg, C. L. (1988). A review of research on picture reading skills of developmentally disabled individuals. *Journal of Special Education* 22:297–329.

Lovaas, I. O. (1981). *Teaching Developmentally Disabled Children: The Me Book*. Texas: Pro-Ed.

———— (1993). The development of a treatment-research project for developmentally disabled and autistic children. *Journal of Applied Behavior Analysis* 26:617–630.

Mahler, M. S. (1968). *On Human Symbiosis and the Vicissitudes of Individuation*. New York: International Universities Press.

———— (1972). *Rapprochement Subphase of the Separation-Individuation Process*. New York: International Universities Press.

Maker, E. (1996). A prominent washington educator maintains character does count. *Litchfield County Times*, March 22, pp. 1, 13–14.

Marshall, R. J. (1979). Countertransference with children and adolescents. In *Countertransference*, ed. L. Epstein and A. H. Feiner, pp. 407–444. New York: Jason Aronson.

McEachin, J. J., Smith, T., and Lovaas, I. O. (1993). Long-term outcome for children with autism who received early intensive behavioral treatment. *American Journal on Mental Retardation* 97(4):359-372.

McGuire, W. (1981). How Jung counseled a distressed patient. *Spring*: 185–191.

Megan, K. (1996). Character counts! Promoting values among state's children. *Hartford Courant*, Oct. 15, pp. A3, A8.

Miller, P. H. (1983). *Theories of Developmental Psychology: Third Edition*. New York: W. H. Freeman.

Millon, T. (1996). *Disorders of Personality: DSM-IV and Beyond*. New York: Wiley.

Minuchin, S. (1978). *Families and Family Therapy*. Cambridge, MA: Harvard University Press.

Mirenda, P. (1986). Covert conditioning. In *Alternatives to Punishment: Solving Behavior Problems with Non-aversive Strategies*, ed. G. W. LaVigna and A. M. Donnellan, pp. 157–176. New York: Irvington.

Mogenson, G. (1992). *Greeting the Angels: An Imaginal View of the Mourning Process*. Amityville, NY: Baywood.

Oaklander, V. (1988). *Windows to Our Children*. Highland, NY: Gestalt Journal Press.

Pfeiffer, S. I., and Baker, B. C. (1994). Residential treatment for children with dual diagnoses of mental retardation and mental disorders. In *When There's No Place Like Home: Options for Children Living Apart from Their Natural Families*, ed. E. D. Balcher. New York: Paul K. Brooks.

Ribi, A. (1990). *Demons of the Inner World: Understanding Our Hidden Complexes*, trans. M. H. Kohn. Boston: Shambhala.

Rosenberg, J. L., and Kitaen-Morse, B. (1996). *The Intimate Couple*. Atlanta: Turner Publishing.

Rosenberg, J. L., Rand, M. J., and Assay, D. (1985). *Body, Self, and Soul*. Atlanta: Humanics Limited.

Rowe, C. E., and Mac Isaac, D. S. (1995). *Empathic Attunement*. Northvale, NJ: Jason Aronson.

Schaefer, C. E., and Swanson, A. J., eds. (1993). *Children in Residential Care*. Northvale, NJ: Jason Aronson.

Scott, D., and Rosentiel, A. (1975). Covert positive reinforcement studies: review, critique, and guidelines. *Psychotherapy: Theory, Research, and Practice* 12:374–384.

Siegel, B. (1996). *The World of the Autistic Child*. New York: Oxford University Press.

Simons, J., and Oishi, S. (1987). *The Hidden Child: The Linwood Method for Reaching the Autistic Child*. Bethesda, MD: Woodbine House.

Simpson, R. (1989). An interview with O. Ivar Lovaas. *Focus on Autistic Behavior* 4(4):1–11.

Spensley, S. (1989). Psychodynamically oriented psychotherapy in autism. In *Diagnosis and Treatment of Autism*, ed. C. Gillberg, pp. 237–250. New York: Plenum.

Tobin, P. T. (1995). Six steps to starting a child sexual abuse prevention program. *NRCCSA News* 4(2):1–5.

Tustin, A. (1980). Autistic objects. *International Review of Psycho-Analysis* 7:27–39.

Tustin, F. (1992). *Autistic States in Children*. London: Routledge & Kegan Paul.

——— (1984). Autistic shapes. *International Review of Psycho-Analysis* 11:279–290.

——— (1986). *Autistic Barriers in Neurotic Patients*. New Haven: Yale University Press.

——— (1988). Psychotherapy with children who cannot play. *International Review of Psycho-Analysis* 15:93–106.

——— (1990). *The Protective Shell in Children and Adults*. London: Karnac.

Valenti-Hein, D., and Schwartz, L. D. (1995). *The Sexual Abuse*

Interview for Those with Developmental Disabilities. Santa Barbara, CA: James Stanfield Co.

Wikler, L., Wasow, M., and Hatfield, E. (1981). Chronic sorrow revisited: parent vs. professional depiction of the adjustment of parents of mentally retarded children. *American Journal of Orthopsychiatry* 51(1).

Williams, D. (1992). *Nobody Nowhere: The Extraordinary Autobiography of an Autistic.* New York: Times Books.

Willis, T. J., LaVigna, G. W., and Donnellan, A. M. (1993). *Behavior Assessment Guide.* Los Angeles: Institute for Applied Behavior Analysis.

Wing, L., Gould, J., Yeates, S. R., and Brierley, L. M. (1977) Symbolic play in severely mentally retarded and in autistic children. *Journal of Child Psychology and Psychiatry* 18:167–178.

Winnicott, D. W. (1986). *Home is Where We Start From.* New York: Norton.

—— (1992). *Playing and Reality.* London: Routledge.

Workman, E. A., and Dickinson, D. J. (1979a). The use of covert conditioning with children: three empirical case studies. *Education and Treatment of Children* 2:245–259.

—— (1979b). The use of covert conditioning in the treatment of a hyperactive child: an empirical case study. *Journal of School Psychiatry* 17:67–73.

Workman, E. A., and Williams, R. L. (1980). Self-cued relaxation in the control of an adolescent's violent arguments and debilitating somatic complaints. *Education and Treatment of Children* 3:315–322.

Yalom, I. D. (1975). *The Theory and Practice of Group Psychotherapy.* New York: Basic Books.

Index